HOW TO BE A PROPERTY DEVELOPER

Alan Bailey's

HOW TO BE A PROPERTY DEVELOPER

MERCURY

First published in 1988
by Mercury Books
Published in paperback 1991
by Mercury Books
Gold Arrow Publications Ltd
862 Garratt Lane, London SW17 0NB

Set in Plantin & Helvetica by Phoenix Photosetting
Printed and bound in Great Britain by
Mackays of Chatham Ltd, Chatham, Kent

British Library in Cataloguing in Publication Data
Bailey, Alan
    How to be a property developer. – New ed.
    I. Title
    332.63

    ISBN 1–85251–115–X

Alan Bailey has been around and about the property industry
for a long time in a number of guises. Few of us have been
able to keep track of all of his interests. Most of us have,
however, heard him on his feet at conferences or dinners, heard
him at meetings on professional subjects and read him in this
or that newspaper or magazine under his own name or a few
pseudonyms. Everyone in property knows that outrageous pair,
Stackup and Gloria, on the back page of *Estates Times* every
week and the other characters he has created in cartoon strips
in half a dozen publications.

Whether standing, sitting, writing or drawing, he can usually
be relied upon to be contentious — and his humour can have
the scatter of a shotgun or the awful precision of a high-velocity
rifle. I have personally suffered from both — but, always a
masochist, I probably have the biggest collection of Stackup
originals outside his own archives. Underneath it all, there is
nevertheless a serious mind — and his wide-ranging consultancy and charitable work underlines the other side of his
nature. He describes himself as a practising schizophrenic.

This book is a mix of the inevitable humour and that under-
lying seriousness. I enjoyed it. Although I have myself been
around for just as long — well, almost — *How to be a Property
Developer* put a new slant on some things I have come to take
for granted. As an introduction to the business, it has rather

more realism than many of the academic tomes most of us had to read to get us going.

The property industry deals in billions — of pounds and square feet of space. The workloadings on developers, contractors and professionals alike are demanding — sometimes overwhelming — but few will admit it. The problems facing government and the industry to improve the fabric on which society relies are, to say the least, formidable. But, despite all this, there should be time for humour in everything.

Sir Christopher Benson
Chairman, MEPC plc

Brook House
Park Lane
Mayfair
W1

ACKNOWLEDGEMENTS

The idea for *How to be a Property Developer* was wrung out of me in order to meet the promotional needs of a client — the Elliott Group of Companies of Bishop's Stortford. A short version in a limited edition was published by the Group in December, 1986, and distributed free to Elliott's clients, customers and friends.

Its success encouraged me, my literary agent Michael Hyde and publisher Robert Postema to believe that a longer, funnier book might have a wide appeal. I am grateful to all of them for their help and encouragement — and, particularly to Christopher Elliott of the Elliott Group who not only took the initial plunge but also had to learn to live with my inability to write anything at all before the eleventh hour.

Stackup, Gloria and the other characters which grace these pages appear every week in strip form in *Estates Times*. I am grateful to David Wicks and Lee Mallett for agreeing to their continued guest appearances.

But, of course, most of all, my thanks are due to the members of the development industry itself — just for being there and doing the things they do, being the people they are and providing me, after years of observation, participation and service, with the necessary background information which makes my commentary possible.

ALAN BAILEY

CONTENTS

INTRODUCTION

It seems that everybody wants to be a developer. Solicitors, accountants, architects, surveyors, ex-cabinet ministers, boy sopranos whose voices have broken, the Church Commissioners, mill owners, ex-boxers and contractors all seem intent to leave some lasting memorial to their wit and ingenuity and to their lasting profit. And, of course, they are not alone. Everybody wants to be a developer.

On the face of it, property development is a creative activity which produces untold riches without obvious effort. Hundreds, probably thousands, of people with no apparent qualifications have made some well-publicised fortunes out of it — almost as big as the fortunes made by pop stars, Steve Davis, call girls, Samantha Fox and those chaps in the Underground who play guitars, mouth-organs or ageing clarinets. It has to be said that all of these other activities require a modicum of talent or an abundance of other marketable physical attributes. Property development, on the other hand, frankly, looks all too easy — for most of the time.

It doesn't even need money. Anybody knows that the financial institutions like the pension funds, the insurance companies, the clearing banks and the Middle Eastern banks are up to here with the stuff. The Japanese have developed a yen for property investment and are, to say the least, bullish. Everyone but everyone with a bit of cash seems anxious to invest it in any wild multi-million pound project dreamed up at the dining-room table.

It is a fact that the dining-room table has been the launching pad for a few property development fortunes. Those fortunes have soared like the occasional successful rocket into space because the true entrepreneurial developer has a knack of keeping his overheads to a minimum in the early years. It is only later — safe in the security of a swollen deposit account and numberless investments in bricks, mortar, glass and cement — that he takes an office and the other trappings of success.

And even when things go wrong, it seems that the bankrupt property developer can usually be found sunning himself in a modest, unassuming little place somewhere west of Cannes. His Picassos are still on the wall and his Rolls is still in the garage — all in his wife's name as is the swimming-pooled villa itself. Of course, she is still sitting at the same dining-room table in the council flat in Balham where it all began. Lord Young of Graffham, himself no mean developer in his day, in his imitation of Supermac, was probably quite right. It is hard to imagine anyone having it quite so good — so long as you are not left at the dining-room table in Balham when it's raining.

But, in fact, there is a catch. This popular image of the property entrepreneur is some distance from reality. In truth, the troubled world of the developer is absolutely littered with bad fairies. They have names like Planning Authority, Professional Fees, Contractors' Claims and Downturn. There is a particularly evil gnome called Short-Term Borrowing who has a continuing and apparently incestuous relationship with his sister, Voids. She has all the transmittable diseases to which the developer is prone such as incipient anxiety neurosis, common planning blight and high-interest herpes. Because of this, the developer is the chap with the fingernails bitten to the quick, a brow etched to the skull with heavy lines, a lovable but all too noticeable tic, overfull ashtrays and a briefcase containing a telephone which rings in public places (it's a wrong number), a half-eaten sandwich, a bottle of heart pills and innumerable site plans of long-gone hopes and opportunities.

His is a story of the might-have-been. His most frequently used sentences start with the words 'If only . . .' A rough statistic, garnered only from years of observation rather than the more reliable sources such as Jones Lang Wootton's Research Department, indicates a development abort-rate of about ninety-five per cent. The abortionists are, of course, those same bad fairies — Planning Authority and his friends — who, at the most critical stages of a project, are invariably joined by slothful Letting Agents and Property Lawyers who gravely mutter words like 'misconceived' and 'misconception'. It is not surprising that the abort-rate is so high when there is so much misconception about.

The remaining five per cent — the projects that succeed — provide the excitement. That five per cent are the cause of that incurable optimism from which all developers and would-be developers suffer. It is a disease endemic in the property industry and provides its driving force — driving the hopeful on to fortune or bankruptcy in roughly equal proportions.

This brief guide to the property industry is intended, first, for the budding property entrepreneur in the hope that he (or she for that matter — on the principle that nothing is free from female interference these days) will be put off by it and hopefully turn towards some other and more gainful employment. After all, the business is already far too overcrowded. It is intended, secondly, and in the hope that it will help them to mend their ways, for those who contribute in one way or another to the property developer's success or failure. These include the architects, the surveyors, the lawyers, the planning authorities, the funding sources — the list is a long one. It even includes the potential tenants who have become as power-conscious as the trade unions thought they were at a time before Thatcher, MacGregor and Murdoch. And, thirdly, it is intended for the developers themselves. The successful can read it as they are driven to the opening ceremony of their next major achievement; the unsuccessful as they lie beside their pools somewhere west of Cannes.

Now read on. It is not entirely serious.

1 SO YOU WANT TO BE A DEVELOPER!

You will all know about the famous developer — described as the daddy of them all — who built a fine and well-known office block in Central London. When it was finished, he didn't let it. Nevertheless, its value increased annually by a sum greater than the loan interest. That building was and is a magnificent failure that glittered with success. It glitters even more now that it has become the headquarters of the Confederation of British Industry. But, more important for our purposes, it was described as obscene — not that its Seifertesque lines were at all obscene but because its capital value grew like Topsy as the rents and values of the buildings around it escalated.

The building became the butt of the conservationist, the preservationist and the anti-developer lobbies. It was held up as a phallic symbol of profit, raping London's interesting but cramped little alleyways, its sordid corners and ageing Georgian, Victorian and Edwardian slums. It became the symbol of the 'property developer' — a name still used by critics in the same breath as 'model' or 'actress' to describe miscreants facing the bench who don't want to own up to what they really do for a living. The property developer — categorised as a kind of latter-day Genghis Khan or Attila the Hun bent on pillaging, looting and destruction — was castigated in the press. The property developer — grown fat on profit and human suffering — was not regarded as a fit person to be invited to respectable dinner parties. The property developer — philistine and filthy rich — was the enemy of the people. The property developer — linked inexorably with names like Rachman (not to mention Christine and Mandy) — lived the life of Riley before even Riley felt he could afford it.

The anti-developer lobby was both vociferous and effective. Pink politicians spat out the words 'property developer' as though those who were so described deserved a place in a leper colony rather than the better reaches of Mayfair and Belgravia. Orchestrated obstruction of even the most reasonable development projects became very fashionable — and the lobbyists stooped to tactics to win which the developers themselves had never dreamed of trying. Public consultation — then a new and frightening dimension in the process of planning control — threw up reasons for refusal which even the London Borough of Southwark would have been hard put to imagine. The late and much loved Lord George Brown imposed his now historic ban on speculative office building, perhaps more as a popular political gesture than a serious economic weapon. Like many carefully considered political decisions, the ban had the dramatic effect of creating a shortage. Shortage, in turn, inevitably creates rarity value — any economist knows that unless, apparently, he or she works for the Department of Economic Affairs as it then was. The result was a rent spiral coupled with the letting of some unlettable buildings as though they were going out of fashion — which, of course, they were for a while. Included among the potential tenants scrambling for the available but diminishing space was the Property Services Agency — known, at that time in the property industry, as the developer's friend.

Often the cry was heard at dinner parties (no, such was the continuing stigma that property developers had not yet been invited to respectable dinner parties. They dined together — great diners are these property people — and talked shop incessantly, struck deals, bemoaned their lot and said . . .) 'Oh, the dear old PSA will take it'. These were, of course, the heady days of BT (before Thatcher) when bureaucracy was in the hands of the new Imperialists. Growth was impressive and, as the parliamentary draftsmen piled new law upon new law, new statutory order upon new statutory order in the Statute Book, demand for office space and unused red tape reached new heights or depths according to the point of view. It was a good time for property developers. But it wasn't to last. The ban was lifted and the development rat race began all over again. This time, the fringe banks — who had always been around with a few millions to help the developers make a few more — became over-excited, over-persuaded, over-heated and over-confident. The fact was, of course, that they were generally under-qualified to make sensible funding judgements. But they made funding judgements just the same — and they were often terribly wrong.

They weren't alone in this fever of activity. The developers themselves went into a welter of work. Too many developers were imitative. If somebody with a reasonably successful reputation and a Rolls-Royce with personalised number plates decided to build an office in a particular town or city, a few others immediately rushed off to do the same. This resulted in over-supply. It wasn't only happening in the United Kingdom. Mainland Europe and the United States of America were the targets too. In fact, one dazed American was heard to say 'My god, we may have won the War of Independence but the Brits are buying the goddamned place back'. It was a situation in which everyone was culpable — the banks, the developers, the local planning authorities, the professional consultants — and the boom just had to be followed by bust.

And the bust came. Many well-publicised property names were declared bankrupt for mind-boggling sums of money. And, of course, many of them had to fly back from that dreary and rather unnerving airport at Nice to attend their court hearings. The Bank of England had to launch the lifeboat to save the fringe banks — and everyone said 'I told you so' when they hadn't said anything of the kind.

Throughout history, developers have gone from boom to bust and back again. Nash, the creator of all those marvellous and elegant terraces, went bankrupt — mind you, not for quite so much as the 1973/4 stock of unfortunates. He also, by the way, had terrible trouble with the conservationists, preservationists and vestedinterestationists who thought rather less of his designs than does the present-day lobby. And, as if that wasn't enough, he also had trouble with his Royal Patron on a number of counts, some of them relevant to his architectural and planning ability. It has to be said that Royal patronage of Mrs Nash was also something of a problem, although matrimonial strife is no stranger to the developers' beds even today. Perhaps more of that later.

But, since those significant years of 1973/4, when property stars fell from the sky like those on a hot night in Alabama, things have changed. Out of the crash was born a new wisdom, a new caution, a new slimmed-down property industry with a highly professional air. Darwin would have recognised the symptoms, of course. The fittest survived and the fittest had been professional all along, so they said. It was the rank amateurs who tumbled. Nevertheless, they had all suffered and there is nothing quite like a bit of suffering to concentrate the mind on ultimate survival.

Everyone sulked for a while. Some investors, particularly the major financial institutions, picked up some choice bargains at knock-down prices and are still counting the profits — to the benefit of their policy-holders, of course. It, nevertheless, took a little time to restore the confidence destroyed by the crash. But only a little time. The problem was that salaries and wages were jogging upwards — and therefore so were all of those premiums or other percentage contributions people had been persuaded to part with for that rainy day. The funds began looking for outlets for this embarrassment of riches.

They were big spenders. But development costs were big too and, as time went on, they got bigger. Some of the more grandiose schemes were soon too expensive for individual funds. Quite apart from that, there came a time when the funds began to look less kindly on property. There is a cycle in these things and bullishness — or even misguided pig-headedness —

in the equities market can provide a haven for funds in preference to the more stable, but less exciting, investments such as property. The property industry has an extraordinary capacity of bobbing up again like an apple in a bucket. The fact that semi-detached funds preferred to trade in second-hand BT shares and that some schemes were too big for one fund to handle seemed to matter not one whit to the property people. Jargon-ridden but always effervescent, the industry hired some tired hack in a back room to invent something to cope with the problem. He called it 'unitisation' — a word which joined the others in the property world's glossary of jargon.

Jargon is important to the industry. It adds a necessary mystique to keep the numbers of competitors down if only because the competitors cannot understand a word anyone is

talking about. As a money-making business, therefore, it
sounds a difficult and unsafe minefield for the ignorant to tread.
The addition of the suffix '-isation' has a particular appeal. A
mostly American affliction, it was recognised as having infinite
deterrent value. It started, probably, with pedestrianisation —
way back in the balmy days of the Civic Trust and Magdalen
Street in Norwich in the 1950s. One of the latest etymological
sins is 'retailisation' — on the principle, perhaps, that, if you
can industrialise something, you can just as well retailise it.
The world waits agog for some trendy residential developer to
bungalowise a field, if that is not contrary to the wishes of the
Green Vote. 'Valumetrics' were invented by a senior lecturer
at the College of Estate Management years ago and, even to
this day, there is great uncertainty about what he was driving
at. An eminent surveyor on the staff of that pillar of prose, the
Department of the Environment, was heard to mutter into his
champagne at yet another property reception 'Look at them
sipping their Perrier water, speaking in Technospeak which no
one else can understand'. It is a trick.

'Nursery units', 'high tech' and 'science parks' have a faint
logic about them but the introduction of words like 'retailisation', 'securitisation', 'unitisation' and 'droplock' (it has
nothing to do with the clippings behind the hairdresser's chair)
are now in common usage in the industry. There are other
devices. A simple enough term like 'tender panel' once meant
a group of chaps sitting round a table with a paper knife to
open sealed tenders for this or that building job. It should still
do so. But, no — tender panel is a method of raising short-
term floating rate finance through a long-term facility at a fixed
interest margin. Well, of course it is — any fool knows that
and, if he doesn't, there is absolutely no place for him in the
property industry.

When the first edition of this book was published, the
property industry was alive and well. Developers — and you
read about them every day in the newspapers — were putting
together proposals of gargantuan size in terms of both floor space

and cost. Of course, the biggest were in London and the prosperous South East. London Docklands is a case in point.

One day, someone will write a book about London Docks. In fact, someone has probably already started. It has all the ingredients of romance, success, disaster and recovery which made Barbara Cartland so successful. It is, however, unlikely that Dame Barbara will tackle the story. There are some parts of Limehouse which are just too raunchy for either her tastes or those of her readers. An epic description of unwashed Lascar seamen walking crab-like from the Docks with little bags of raw opium strapped to their crotches would, in any event, be enough to turn off even the most dedicated hophead. The story of Docklands is infinitely more exciting. The Isle of Dogs, Wapping and even the old Becton Gas Works — they have a ski slope there now — all have a story to tell.

In 1980, the London Docklands Development Corporation — a body created by statutory device to outwit a bunch of recalcitrant local authorities — surveyed its lot. And a fairly sordid lot it was. Everyone had been talking about it for years — even before the Docks themselves ceased to operate. Little had been done — at least, little that was constructive. Some of the docks were filled in to meet the provisions of some now forgotten plan — and, in 1986, they were being unfilled to satisfy the pent-up demand for waterside property. But the real story of Docklands is the attraction of enormous public and private investment to regenerate its heart. It is success at a million pounds plus an acre.

Indeed, so successful is it that the business City of London is nervous that it will be replaced as the world's leading financial centre by the People's Republic of Southwark. Competition from New York, Tokyo, Hong Kong or Paris is bad enough but to have the competition on your doorstep or just across the bridge is serious. In consequence, an essentially preservationist plan for the City of London was amended in an attempt at self-assertion — although how a preservationist plan could be fashioned in the first place by the planning committee which permitted the Lloyds building is hard to understand. With any luck, the shockwaves from the Big Bang, the October 1987 crash and the 1990 recession will eventually blow it down.

Public investment in Docklands primed the pump. Private investment has flowed well ever since. Houses, factories, offices, communications — all improved, all bubbling along but with allegedly equal emphasis on the community and jobs. It is the acceptable face of capitalism — so long as they keep getting it right.

Getting it right is not always easy. Olympia and York, a not insignificant development organisation of international renown, is building the biggest, tallest, best equipped, most modern office complex ever imagined down there on the 'Isle of Dogs'. Rents are lower than those in the City of London — and, since Saatchi and Saatchi went mad and paid through the nose for Landsdowne House in Berkeley Square, lower than the West End too. In consequence, some large organisations have reserved their space, measured in acres of Wilton broadloom. There are still many acres to let. Canary Wharf — the name derives from bananas rather than songbirds — is a prime example of just how difficult it is to get things right. The construction period of such mega-developments is so extended that it can run through several booms and several busts before it is finished. You can wear out a lot of worry beads in ten years.

One of the features of recent property history is the co-operation which exists between the public and private sectors. It has existed for a long time. Even in the 1950s, some of the more progressive local authorities saw the likely benefits of sharing the developers' cake. Local authorities had, by dint of being local authorities, become sizeable landowners in their own right in their central areas. They were also the planning authority, the highway authority and the authority for this or that function — all highly relevant to central area redevelopment. This gave them an edge in negotiating the construction of shopping centres and any crumbs of planning gain that might fall from the developers' tables.

The success of the progressives persuaded the rest that capitalism had its advantages — even if you happened to be devoted Marxists or Militants. Derek Hatton is probably writing a book about it. And so the joint venture became almost standard practice. Local authorities no longer have to be satisfied with the crumbs. They enjoy fruity slices of profit — and their electorates enjoy shopping facilities of the highest standards in controlled climates and with fast foods of infinite international variety welling out of their plastic containers at the drop of a fiver.

Not just shopping, of course. New libraries, car parks, bus stations — all under the guise of planning gain — are adjuncts to the centres and the subject of considerable civic pride. For the councillors themselves, pride is justified on two counts — the facility itself and the hard-nosed negotiations which created it. The local authorities, although not the fastest on their feet — particularly when it comes to granting planning permission — saw the benefits of jumping onto the developers' bandwagon. The medium for this local government equivalent to piracy was and is known as Section 52 — although the number of the Section has changed under a new Act. It will, at the end of their days, be carved on the headstones of a hundred developers. 'It was Section 52 what did for him' they might say. Once it was the Black Death.

The financial institutions — once slow and cumbersome themselves — had helped a few property entrepreneurs along the road to financial success. It dawned on their consciousness in time that they too could share the cake. And not only share it. They could have it and eat it too. They had the money. They could buy the expertise and bring it in-house. They could take all the profit. Direct development by the funds is now common enough to be unexceptional — and very good at it they are too.

The contractors — those who actually built all of this expensive real estate at a declining mark-up — also saw the light. Many formed property development companies. Some of them were rich in resources and, as if that were not competition enough for the developers, were fairly confident that their contracting arms could actually put up the buildings at a modest profit. This caused some sharp intakes of breath when local authorities were involved in the development — which they sometimes were, of course. Tenders had to be invited and it is a fact worthy of a thesis that, somehow, the contractor arm of the development company managed to offer the lowest price.

While all of this was going on, there was no diminution in the number of whizz-kids determined to take their places in the ranks of property entrepreneurs. Despite the obvious competition, despite the increasing expertise necessary to make projects tick, despite the fact that the investing institutions blew very cold after blowing hot for ages — despite all of these things, the clamour at the entrepreneurial door was incessant. And, of course, it still is.

It has to be said that not all those who knock and are admitted stay inside the property world for very long. They have, as they say, their entrances and their exits — usually towards the bankruptcy courts or to Mile End to explain to the little woman where the life savings have gone. It is not difficult to fail. In fact, it is not difficult to fail and fail and fail again. There are several people who are extravagantly skilful at failure. It has become an art form — that look of pained surprise when failure happens yet again. It would be wrong — indeed reckless — to name them but the property world knows who they are and takes them out to lunch occasionally for old times' sake.

But not all is failure. There are always new ideas. Yet another eminent surveyor said, ages ago, that all the best industrial sites had been developed. His opinion overlooked the fact of the expanding motorway network. The M25 has thrown up a string of sites suitable for manufacture or distribution — or for that late 1980s phenomenon, the retail park.

There is always something new. For a long time, many

people were saying that fun had to be introduced into the world of shopping. Shopping — or retailing as the property world has it — was once a high street scramble. Shoppers dodged each other, vehicles, those sharp bits of metal that held up awnings, cascading water from defective blinds and vehicles, always more vehicles, in conditions which no one found attractive. Housewives fought bravely through the weekly chore and strong men flinched away from any invitations to join the family shop on Saturday afternoons. The sheer awfulness of shopping was one of the reasons for the extraordinary demand for allotments in the immediate post-war years. Men had found their excuse to avoid the weekly excursion to the shops.

But things were to change. It started with pedestrianisation. That, at least, began to limit the war between shoppers and cars. Nevertheless, high street shopkeepers believed that it would sound the death knell of the high street and, more importantly and more immediately, affect their profits. People, they said, would go to the corner shop near which they could park. It didn't work out like that. In fact, people preferred the relative calm of the pedestrianised streets — there was one less hazard to dodge. As car ownership increased, that hazard alone could have overwhelmed the traditional high street. After pedestrianisation, high street shopkeepers found benefits they had not imagined — but there was always a battle before it was introduced.

And then came the covered malls, the air conditioning, the forests of potted plants, the seating areas, even the occasional pub. Architecturally-designed sheds had entrances which led into new shopping paradises. And things became even more elaborate, more sophisticated. The Americans and the French had an influence which was reflected in imported ideas which should have had no place in the United Kingdom. They made shopping fun. The kids could play on an assortment of rides and models in a fairytale world. Fast food courts fed shoppers a variety of ethnic take-aways — probably with the exception of that handiest of convenience foods, the Cornish pasty, although it has at last become established alongside the Chinese take-away, the donor kebabs, the beefburger and hot dog. Fun had, at last, been brought to shopping.

Someone, of course, had to go one better. In the chilly North East, an enterprising entrepreneur saw the benefits of the enterprise zone and decided to bring shopping to fun. The Metrocentre was born which served up goods with the whizz-bang-whollop of an amusement park. Any reluctant father refusing to take part in the fun could be set apart from the herd — total family shopping was in; the allotments were finally out. You can see them from train windows — weed-covered and neglected — ripe, one day, for redevelopment as starter homes or sheltered housing. The trends produced a new description — the retail warehouse. Goods, piled high, were cheap by jowl as though Aladdin's cave had been done over by the Seven Plastic Gnomes — a pantomime of retailing in which everyone takes part. And it won't stop there.

In fact, it hasn't. The leisure industry has decided to pick up where retailing might be persuaded to leave off. The theme park with or without pretentions towards Disneyland brings a new dimension to merchandising — even to the extent of manufacturing on site to cut down on distribution costs.

All of this underlines the extraordinary ability of the property industry to adapt and bring in new ideas which the public never dreamed they wanted. Industrial and warehousing properties are a case in point. At the turn of the century, a chap called Ebenezer Howard had the notion to segregate housing from industry. He created the garden cities — and the whole of the new towns movement, starting in 1948 or so, stemmed from Ebenezer. Industry should not impose itself on housing. No longer should workers' hovels cluster round dark satanic mills. The houses should go there and the industry should go there — resulting, of course, in acres of expensive tarmacadam which was used twice a day by a frantic workforce rushing from home to work and back again. Industrial estates became industrial parks — the difference was a conifer or two — and then some wag saw the rise of the microchip and realised its full potential. Buildings had to be flexible, adaptable, to meet the needs of the new technologies. They had to have mixed uses to bring together invention, manufacture and distribution all in elastic buildings which could expand, contract, heighten and lower but with ample car-parking because the workforce was intellectual and demonstrably well-to-do. And so high tech was born. Suddenly, everything was high tech. Industrial sites with algae growing on the 'to let' boards were given a lick of paint, a new name and an adjective or two and became science parks overnight. Once again, the property industry showed its flexibility, adaptability and elasticity.

Mind you, it was doing this at a time when a host of pundits had decided that the segregation of housing, shops and industry was perhaps not such a good thing after all.

Everyone knows that no one can be right all of the time. When things are moving fast, it is difficult to be right even some of the time. Local authorities, pension funds, insurance companies, developers and would-be developers, planners, architects, surveyors — yes, they've all got it wrong at some time or another. What is interesting is that only the developers and would-be developers are truly vulnerable.

You will remember that the chapter began with a written hollow laugh — so you want to be a developer! He is the chap in the middle of all this. Local authorities get it wrong for one reason or another and they get re-elected. The pension funds and insurance companies can't cope with all the money rolling into their coffers and turn to buying estate agencies or creating trendy financial services groups. And we know what has happened to them. The planners — well, it is difficult to be sure what they are up to but there is, they say, a shortage of them so they are safe enough. Some harsh words have been said about architects but, like the surveyors, they charge fees whether disaster has struck, is about to strike or will certainly strike during the life cycle of the building. Some wag is now trying to make designers responsible for design faults

for ever. It's the developer who is stuck as piggy in the middle, carrying the risk, the can, the odium and the protests of the preservationist lobby etched on his heart.

Even if he wends his way through the development jungle and his building rises proudly over London or Swindon or wherever it may be, the chances are that someone will squat in it. And if he actually lets it, someone will note the sudden surge in profitability and the developer will find his shares being snapped up by some non-property giant bent on being — what — yes, you have it — bent on being a developer.

It was always so. Recent history merely repeats the saga of change, innovation and just rank rotten luck which those who have developed have suffered over the centuries.

2 OTHER RELEVANT HISTORY

Of course, the history of development didn't only start in the 1950s with the end of wartime building licensing. Ever since man came down from the trees or up from the slime and realised that nights could be both chilly and dangerous, he has sought or created shelter — shelter either from the elements or from beasts of prey and usually both. And shelter, let it be said, has never come cheap. Primitive man often had to fight for his cave — dispossessing two or four legged occupants with a swing of the club as opposed to a notice under the Landlord & Tenant Act. Some landlords still have a sneaking preference for the old ways.

Even caves had degrees of desirability. First or second floor accommodation up the cliff face was invariably preferred to the ground floor which always seemed vulnerable to the passing attentions of mammoths and sabre-toothed tigers which similarly sought shelter. Caves with little nooks in which possessions might be stored or even hidden were at a premium — just as today the merest hint of a shelf or a fitted cupboard or two adds immeasurably to the mortgage requirement. A natural funnel system which cleared both the smoke from the fires and the odours from the unwashed neolithic was something to be coveted, fought for and defended. It is interesting to note that controlled climates are still fought over — some want the heating up, some want it down and some want it not at all, preferring an open window and the right to freeze to death or expire from heatstroke depending on the time of year.

As man created structures in the form of settlements, he

soon discovered that all men were not the same — not to mention the women who were obviously and subtly different even with body hair. Men were adept at this and that — at different things. Some were fleet of foot and could hunt successfully, bringing home the bacon in huge quantities until religion began to influence their eating habits. Others could make things — like wheels, houses and weapons. The idea of barter slowly dawned on thinning and broadening skulls and, soon, chaps were swapping joints of woolly bear for flint axes, bone needles or simply help with the roof. Man-to-man bartering quickly — ten thousand years or so to be precise — matured into markets. There was no stopping us then.

Man became ambitious. One man may have had more possessions than another; even more wives. Covetous eyes were turned on what he had and possessions began to indicate wealth and standing. Two-storeyed huts were sought after — not necessarily because the domestic animals could shelter in the lower floors but because they were a sure sign of success. Flamboyance was in; simplicity was out. As the French primitives said 'Plus ça change, plus c'est la même chose' — and, of course, they still do.

All of this was a precursor to present-day uniformity of style. But, in the early years, people didn't cart building materials all over the world. If they were importing or exporting anything at all, they preferred the exotic — like gold and spices, silks and perfumes. People used what was available locally for building purposes and adapted it to a form suitable for living. The plains Indians of North America sewed together a few buffalo hides, stretched them over some supple timber and daubed paint over them and themselves to make the whole environment both colourful and practical. As the herds of bison moved on to greener pastures, the Indians merely rolled up their tepees and went after them. It is the origin of the expression 'up sticks'.

Eskimos had never heard of Italian marble. They used what they had in abundance as a means of creating shelter — just as the Indians had done although there is no record of Eskimos ever resorting to paint. What they used was snow — and the hole outside the front door was the larder.

Stilt houses were essentially practical in areas prone to flood,

venomous snakes and termites. Communities which had tamed their cattle found that dung had adhesive and weatherproofing qualities not possessed by mud. They also found that the thorn bomas made well-endowed lions think twice before attempting a leap after a plump heifer or an even plumper wife. It was all essentially practical.

But civilisation was creeping up on us. Even in those days, developers were enjoying experimentation — dabbling in new ideas. The Hanging Gardens of Babylon resulted, it is said, from an excessive fondness for window-boxes on the part of Nebuchadnezzar or one of his successors — a precursor to the modern atrium with which some architects now hide their lack of detailing.

The Pyramids are probably one of the best examples of human development flamboyance. Admittedly, the Pharaohs had the notion that they were gods and, although the rest of us have remained largely unconvinced, they made a stab at architectural immortality at least through the building of tombs which do absolutely nothing for the Saharan skyline. Some architects today have similar reputations. But in those days, the practice of architecture was a risky one. If an architect was chosen to design a pyramid for some sickening Pharaoh, there was an odds-on chance that he would find himself bricked up inside it so that the secret of access would die with him. It is a sad truth that estate agents, faced with the prospect of marketing hideous and unlettable buildings in areas of over-supply, wish the architects, the developers and everyone connected with them much the same fate.

Since sophistication began, things have gone wrong with buildings for one reason or another. There is, inevitably, a gap between ambition and the harsh reality of building economics. Every developer knows that. In consequence, after the ecstasy of conception, realism creeps in insidiously in the form of savings here, cheese-paring there. It is a bit like sex and parent-hood. It is likely that the tower — the campanile — at that church in Pisa would never have leaned at all if the quantity surveyors hadn't insisted that the piling was cut to a minimum just to save a lira or two on the capital cost. The world has been richer in consequence. Professional howlers abound throughout the ages without even the excuse of high alumina cement.

Development was a fairly cosy affair until someone invented planning. Human settlements grew, not in any orderly way based on the present American system of straight lines and lots, but haphazardly, without order. Growth was not, of course, without purpose. If some industrial baron built a mill with a view to profit, he also built millworkers' houses around it in a convenient cluster, presumably on the principle that it saved bus fares and he had a fair chance of getting the work-force on the job as the whistle blew. In no time at all, some enterprising wife of a tenant opened a shop in her front parlour which no one used anyway. The area soon had the essentials of a commercial entity including what were very basic leisure facilities like the Working Men's Club, the Methodist Chapel Mothers' Union and the works outing to Seaburn.

In the grander places, like Mayfair and Belgravia, which came along much later, a conscious decision was taken by the architects not to build back-to-back. Central squares with trees and flowers were created to face fine terraces of elegant buildings. The Belgravia format, for example, proved very popular among the well-to-do largely because the Prince Regent had decided to make Buckingham House into a palace. It has to be said that successive generations of the Royal Family have been trying ever since and it still isn't a patch on Versailles or even the Kremlin.

The North/South divide is no innovation. The apparent cramped squalor of the industrialised areas was frowned upon by the reformers. Even those who had themselves built the cramped squalor didn't like it very much and invented good reasons to escape from it — at a profit. St Annes on the Sea, for example, was the dream of a few millionaires from Lancashire — a healthy haven, free from the smoke, noise, dust and the workers themselves. They obviously used the same rule and T-square as those used to design most of New York because the little town still has the straight roads, criss-crossing at intersections, and mostly the same imaginative street names. It took an age to get the project off the ground and near-bankruptcy threatened on several occasions.

Nash, of course, was a master planner, architect and builder — and anyone who studies his ideas will appreciate his vision. His vision was not always implemented but enough of what he did remains to act as a balance to the work of some of his professional and less talented successors. Where Nash made his mistake was in being a jack of all trades. If he had stuck to his planning and his architecture and left the building contracting alone, he wouldn't have gone bankrupt. Any latter-day contractor could have told him that. It is a matter of fact that, as contractors are quick to remind anyone who will listen, architects and planners rarely go bankrupt. In fact, the more they spend of their clients' money, the more they earn. Contractors have somehow failed to achieve this happy relationship with their clients — indeed, so far as it is possible to judge, they have failed to achieve that happy relationship with anyone else up or down the development hierarchy. It is the old story of the professional conspiracy against the simple honest tradesman.

As we have said, the man who is or was at the roots of the present planning system was one Ebenezer Howard who invented the garden city. He disliked the squalor of the mill towns where factory chimneys poured soot and sulphur over the local inhabitants. Mind you, he preferred to build his garden cities in the prosperous and more rural South East and places like Letchworth and Welwyn are the result. He segregated the residential, commercial and industrial buildings — with the industrial element tucked neatly in the North-East corner so that the factory smoke could be whisked by the South West variables to choke the cows and sheep which lay in the windward direction.

Segregation is a human folly based almost entirely on the class system. It is a sign of success or position to settle onself apart from the crowd — hence the executive loo, the cellular system of offices or even Hampstead. But animal instincts are just the reverse. It is when elephants or buffalo get weak that they are set aside from the herd. In truth, human instincts are much the same. When Ebenezer Howard's garden city ideas were transposed into the post-war New Towns movement, no one who was asked doubted that the idea was a good one. But no one actually asked the people — and many of them thought that they had been set aside from their workplaces, the shops and the delightful development hotch-potch they once called home. Words like sterile were used to describe their new town environments — and many crept back to the cosy smoke.

There were other influences — as there had been throughout history. This time it was female emancipation and even transcendence. Some women had always proved to be troublesome — for quite different reasons — like Boadicea, Cleopatra and Mrs. Thatcher. But shifts in world economics put many women in the role of bread winners as opposed to slicers. They were quite happy to work in their light industrial units so long as they weren't too far from home or the shops. Light industry, shops and houses began to merge again and some of the proponents of the New Towns' way of things began to doubt if Ebenezer Howard had been right in the first place. Governments have indicated that mixed uses might not be such a bad thing after all and all kinds of encouragement are now being given to imaginative and compatible uses close together.

But humanity is a paradox. On the one hand, there are the masses who, because of some innate insecurity, like to huddle together in close proximity in what the pressure groups refer to as settlements on a human scale. On the other hand, there are those very individual persons who want to go one better. Taller skyscrapers, bigger shopping centres (and, of course, more luxurious) and office building complexes so large that it is easy to become bemused and confused by the number of noughts in the floorspace calculations.

Don't blame the architects. It is the clients — be they public or private — who are the decision-makers. In fact, one of the problems is that the decision-makers keep on making decisions once they are supposed to have made up their minds. Designs are changed, specifications are altered, needs are reassessed. The whole development business — and the wealth of professional people and contractors (particularly contractors) — has grown out of all proportion to the world's needs simply because everyone seems to enjoy making the building process more complicated. The Pyramids, the Parthenon, large parts of Paris and most of Rome are classic cases of over-development. Only the American government could have commissioned an architect to design a building — the Pentagon — which requires a road map to discover which cloakroom you are entitled to use in accordance with your security grading.

But small and homely building has made as much a mark on history as the big and flamboyant. If the back streets of

Naples can produce Sophia Loren and Gina Lollobrigida, you can keep the Appian Way.

The future is, however, uncertain. History, which could

once be relied upon to repeat itself, is unlikely to provide the pointers we need. The reason is that people are now subject to a new and serious influence — television. The average serf in the Middle Ages was hardly aware that his particular baron enjoyed a breakfast that would have fed the serf's family for a year if he had had a refrigerator to keep it in. The average serf didn't know about silken sheets, perfumes and plumbing — or, indeed, that the wealthy had another room to sleep in. But they know now.

How the other half lives is common knowledge. Series like *Dynasty* and *Dallas* feed the imaginations and aspirations of the viewers — who also happen to work in offices, factories and shops. They want an office like J R Ewing's. Managers begin to yearn for a secretary like J R Ewing's secretary. And the secretaries want offices like J R Ewing's secretary has and, worse,

bosses like J R Ewing. This has resulted in the use, quite
properly, of words like 'prestigious' to describe office buildings. Marbled lobbies into which it is possible to fit a small
cathedral are now commonplace in London — and, in New
York, the cathedral doesn't have to be particularly small.

Quite apart from the luxury of space, carpeting and
furnishings, people now expect air-conditioning, coloured telephones, car parking spaces and no more than five people to a
loo. This unreasonable spurt in human aspirations is driving
managers to distraction. But, having made the effort both to
understand and afford high technology (invariably bought
before the price dropped 300 per cent), they might have
expected to save a bit of space. Staff reduction and space saving
were stated objectives of high technology or so the computer
advertisers had us believe. As rent and rate levels soared, those
objectives of real savings in overheads had something of an
appeal to those in pursuit of profit. But no — smaller staffs
filled the available space, putting their expensive knees under
even more expensive desks and grinding their stilettos into the
best Wilton — provided by the developers, of course, as an
excuse for a higher rent.

It is difficult to forecast where it will all end. It is common
knowledge that, if a creative advertising agency invents its
own wild concept of a twenty-first-century environment to
sell something mundane like breakfast cereals or saucepans,
everybody wants one. Not the cereals or the saucepans, of
course, but the twenty-first-century environment. The pace is
being forced not by need but by a greed for change among the
majority.

And change is accelerating all the time. The leap from
airships to Concorde in eighty years, from the Fairey Swordfish
to the Space Shuttle in fifty — these are nothing compared
with the leap in accommodation standards given and expected
in the offices, factories, high tech emporia and shopping centres
which the developer once provided and still now provides.
Buildings regarded as advanced in the 1960s are either being

refurbished at twice or three times the original cost or measured for demolition and total redevelopment.

None of this, let it be said, is the fault of the developer. He is merely the instrument to satisfy this lust for higher and higher standards. As we have said before, it was always so. There was always a patron who wanted to build something bigger, something better than his neighbour's. There was always someone with the gift of work ready to commission a bigger hut, a bigger compound, a bigger castle — it was always so throughout history. Now the patron is the masses with their demands for higher standards, better quality and bigger desks in bigger solitary offices with oak coatstands and individual executive toys.

The developer has to meet all these demands. It would be reasonable to expect that, with the pent-up demand for increasing luxury, his job is easy. You wouldn't believe what it is really like.

3 FINDING THE SITE

The fact that there are over sixty million acres of land in the United Kingdom must come as something of a surprise to the average developer. He is heard daily muttering about the serious shortage of land for this or that purpose, demanding its release for development as though it was a stored commodity eked out like the rations so that it lasts for the next millennium. After all, what the developer wants is only his rightful acre, preferably next to the Bank of England.

Land is extraordinary stuff. Apart from occasional patches of erosion, floods, earthquakes and volcanic eruptions on the debit side and modest reclamation on the other (apart from the Dutch, of course, who are terribly clever at it), land is permanent and static. It doesn't usually do anything. It just is — and is done to according to the needs or whims of the people who own it, rent it or have some insolent, statutory right over it such as the government, local authority or British Gas who dig it up constantly. There is therefore no shortage of land — land just is.

This was recognised a long time ago by the draftsmen of sundry property and planning acts. They knew that land was immutable, immovable, and, other than in exceptional circumstances, could not be manufactured. It was far too rigid a substance to be the subject of law. It was, in fact, a law unto itself. So the planners invented land use — a legalistic football which has been kicked about ever since with more energy even than that shown by the Argentinians. Parliamentary draftsmen also invented other influences on land such as restrictive covenants, mineral rights, rights of light, tree preservation orders, common land (there is no common land in Belgravia; well, there wouldn't be, would there?) and a whole list of other things which stop people doing those things to the land which they really want to do.

So what the developer is saying when he bemoans the shortage of land is that there is no land free of restriction on which he can build his Centre Point, Green Giant, Canary Wharf or executive home. Finding a site among all those sixty million acres, taming the jungle of law and restriction which surrounds the use of it, hacking a path to permission — these things have become the first hurdle the developer has to jump in his race to profit. Race is, perhaps, the wrong word. It is usually a slow and tedious trek. The magnet of Brent Cross, that popular shopping emporium on the North Circular road, took seventeen years from the time it was a twinkle in the developer's eye to the time it was opened to an astonished public. Many of them, nearing middle age as the idea was forming, were drawing their old age pensions by the time it was built and some had long since gone to that other shopping centre in the sky which, being in Heaven, you can bet your life, didn't need planning permission.

So the budding developer shouldn't just go and buy any old piece of land. Mind you, some of them do. Some of them have been known to create what is laughingly called a landbank of sites most of which have been bought at 'hope' value. Hope is something that the serious, experienced developer disregards. That, he will say, is for the birds — particularly in the quest for planning permission. He is not entirely hopeless, of course. He will hope that his Grade I listed building will blow down or burn up in the night. He will hope that the planning officer, who never designed a building in his life, won't want to make a start offering design ideas about his. He will hope that his building, whatever and wherever it is, will be built on time at an approximate average of the various cost forecasts given to him by his quantity surveyor during the currency of the contract.

But hope is not a strong element in the make-up of a developer. This, because of the nature of his work, is something of a paradox. It is faith he has — faith in his ability ultimately to beat the system. It is his driving force. He fires it by the employment of teams of experts who spend much of their time trying to outdo the same smartypants parliamentary draftsmen who have tried to tie the developer down in the first place. Fees for professional advice, professional appearances, expert witnesses and aspirin can be as much as thirty per cent of a project cost in a bad case of incipient planning constipation. And there is a lot of it about.

One eminent developer once said that all the best sites for industrial development had gone. He had failed to take into account the motorway programme or, in due course, the Channel Tunnel. Multi-million pound public enterprises of this kind throw up sites like tinsel at Christmas and lucky landowners normally think it is. Good communications are, these days, an essential for good industrial development and the brighter developer had his finger on opportunity before the planning officer had finished his cornflakes at breakfast.

The secret of site finding is imagination and opportunism. That little man seen chasing the fire engine on some urgent call is unlikely to be a press photographer after a scoop. He is likely to be a developer chasing his next urban site. Although it is probably as apocryphal as any developer stories go, it is well known that one embryo developer in the war years carried out his fire-watching duties with a map and notebook on which he noted the sites of the greatest devastation. He struck — and struck his deals — before the smoke had cleared or the dust had settled. That is opportunism on the grandest and most commendable scale — although it has to be said that opportunist fire-watching is unlikely to be a feature of civil defence in World War III.

Another characteristic of the successful developer is his inexorable patience. The purchase of a lease here, a lease there, the covert acquisition of freeholds, the professed encouragement to tenants to depart and, suddenly, there is a site for redevelopment. Buying land with 'hope' value and allowing the goats to continue to graze while the fourteenth amendment to the Structure Plan and the Village Plan are considered by the Minister requires patience of a kind. But the patient task of urban land assembly is a masterly art — particularly if you can do it without someone smelling a rat. If someone does and slips into the action by acquiring a key building or plot, he can cause a great deal of heartache. 'Holding out' is nothing to do with Oliver and his empty bowl. For the holder of the land which is the key to a development site, it is the fast road to fortune.

Clever developers play this game all the time. And, of course, clever developers or their agents can sniff out a promising site or building just as a thirsty elephant smells a waterhole. In truth, there is development opportunity everywhere — but it is not visible to everyone. The best developers have all-seeing eyes and are fed by all-seeing agents from all corners of the map. The brash upstart is unlikely to have the skill. What he will have, of course, is all the opportunities being hawked around by the agents which the established developers have discarded as development rubbish.

It would be wrong to avoid a mention of that site-finding device known as asset stripping. This was a popular description for takeover bids in the 1960s and early 1970s. A clever entrepreneur, sitting at the inevitable dining-room table or, in some cases, in his penthouse suite in Park Lane, would examine the total assets of a target company. He would judge the value of the company not by the number of employees in work, the turnover or the profit but by its assets in the form of land and buildings. The target company might own the freehold of a plum site which lay in an area for which high demand for modern industrial space could be foreseen. The profits from redevelopment would easily outweigh the profits from investment in the company as a going concern. The rest is history and there are a few thousand extra unemployed to prove it.

Even this is no longer exploitable in the way it was. Companies have become much more aware of the value of their property assets — in part at least through the assortment of stories in

the newspapers about asset stripping and the lifestyles of the strippers. Few opportunities of the old kind now exist — and if they do, they have been assessed and discarded by those who know.

It would be wrong to give the impression that the art of asset stripping has been entirely lost. Currently, we are enjoying — again if that is the right word — a boom in the takeover business. Takeovers are an extraordinary phenomenon because nobody seems to lose by them. On the contrary, everybody seems to make heaps of money — particularly the merchant banks, the brokers, the lawyers and the valuers. Those who have been taken over often end up so weighed down with gold that they can look around to take over someone else — much to the delight of the merchant banks, the brokers, the lawyers and the valuers. On the other hand, those taken over can, if they wish, simply just slip away in their newly-acquired yachts and moor them somewhere pleasant.

It is interesting that very few of them actually do that. It may be something to do with the power game. Psychologists probably have an explanation for it but it seems that, once somebody has tasted leadership, power, business-expense lunches at The Ritz or The Savoy — or even The Connaught where you really do have to be somebody — and all those other things that go with a substantial equity share, he or she just can't give it up. Power is addictive — much worse than smoking cocaine or fantasising about Sophia Loren. Even the well-known crooks who retire young to the Costa del Sol after some spectacular heist can't just relax with a long drink and a cool blonde. In no time at all, they are organising away-days to Morocco returning laden to the gunwales with high quality hashish for onward shipment to New York or Bournemouth — wherever the market may currently be the most buoyant and the most profitable.

But the takeover game is with us and the takers-over know that they can trade on some of the assets at a profit. They can trade on for re-development. If they are picking up four hundred outlets in a shops chain, they might merge interests and throw up a large pile of surplus space which they can sell — or use as sites for new buildings, relying either on the ten per cent rule (we'll come to that later) or an easy-going planning authority. All of this is splendid work for the valuers and all the other professionals who seem to be doing rather well out of it. As I say, generally, there seem to be no losers. There are, of course, those among us who try to be a bit too clever — whether making or defending bids — and they lose reputations. They rarely actually lose money in any quantity — and, by the standards of normal mortals, remain filthy rich.

Motorways may have thrown up hundreds of sites — but the fickleness and unpredictability of public taste have thrown up even more. This is the age of two things — retailing and leisure. Eminent surveyors who are given to this kind of thing make serious prognostications about retailing opportunities and needs, mostly in the hope that someone will give them instructions to make the possible happen. There is, for example, the matter of what are now called metrocentres. Anyone with any sense of development history will know that, in the old days, we just had shops. They then graduated into arcades which was a tidy way of making profit out of back land. Arcades became malls and then we had centres. While all this was going on, we went through markets, supermarkets, hypermarkets and superstores. Now, we have metrocentres — the invention of a developer who had the incredibly clever wheeze of slipping a mixed shopping and leisure development into an enterprise zone which gave him all kinds of benefits — including the avoidance of the need for planning permission. The idea was good. For a long time, many of the pundits had been saying that fun should be brought into shopping. That is exactly what the first metrocentre had done or is doing. The eminent surveyors now believe that we need at least five metrocentres on the M25 around London — on the assumption that umpteen retail warehouses — the latest fad — don't get there first.

Retail warehouses are large stock-filled sheds where people buy goods cheaply, spending twice as much as they intended to spend in the first place because the human will is weak and the kids finger the strategically-placed sweets and chocolate bars at the checkout points. Everybody wants a retail warehouse or metrocentre these days. Stately home owners stare knowingly at their rolling parklands dreaming that, one day, they will be filled with avid Asda or Tesco shoppers wheeling their trolleys to the 4000-space car park, picking up Granny on the way who has been at the bingo which is only one of the local attractions.

And, of course, we now have retail parks. These are a conglomeration of retail warehouses containing compatible and complementary trades. They are served by acres of car-parking and provide ancillary delights such as playgrounds for the kids. They are usually well landscaped and, although the buildings are just very large retail sheds, they have, in many cases, been designed by architects and made to look attractive. The main attractions are, however, the car-parking and the location — simple accessibility. There is a pleasure in driving round a ringroad and parking your 1600cc shopping basket close to the checkout points — leaving some paid hand to push your discarded trolley back to where it belongs. Unless you take it back to display your geraniums on your patio, of course! A lot of people do that.

A 1990s phenomonon is the megacentre. Several of these have now appeared. There is Lakeside in Thurrock, for example. Built on near-virgin land — yes beside a lake — it contains no less than one million five hundred thousand square feet of retail space. It has cost £300,000,000 and covers 150 acres. There is parking for 9,000 cars and a 250 space coach park. There is a new £22,000,000 link road joining the M25 to the centre — and that in itself, must be some kind of first. No other private developer has, so far as I know, ever spent 22 million quid of his own money on a public highway. But the vital statistic is that it sits within one hour's drive of 13 million people.

Meadowhall, just outside Sheffield, is another mega-centre — this one a mere million square feet. It has parking for 11,000 cars, a 'bus station' that can take 120 buses at the same time and a coach park for 300 — coaches, not people. They say that 874,000 people live within an easy 15 minutes drive, 2.2 million within the half-hour and 9 million — the long distance people — within the hour. Merryhill, near Dudley, has 1.8 million square feet of shops, free parking for 10,000 motor cars, a coach park for 500 — again coaches, not people — and £20 million has been spent on a monorail system for the happy shoppers. There is a 10-screen cinema complex seating 2,500 and acres of eating places for a range of fast foods and proper meals if you prefer them. Merryhill minibuses cover a seven mile radius using 15 different routes. The centre provides a children's play area, courtesy wheel chairs and a fun programme of mall entertainments.

All of that probably means the four centres — if we include the metrocentre in the North-East — are probably sufficient to serve virtually the whole population of England. Since Lakeside Thurrock was opened in late October 1990, they do say that the car park has been 90 per cent full during shopping hours.

What all of this will do to the traditional high street and the expensive shopping malls in existing centres is difficult to forecast. Ultimate bankruptcies in central locations could yield some prime sites for the earnest searcher — but for what? If all the retailing has been pushed out to the fringes into metro-centres, megacentres, retail warehouses, superstores and retail parks, what will we do with all the space in the central areas? It is a sorry fact that the big demand in central areas is still for car parking space. Car ownership has grown dramatically in the last twenty years and is still growing. Once, a car was a means for taking Mum to the seaside at weekends. Now, it is, at best, a shopping basket. No one goes shopping without a car and that is why car parking space is so important to the metrocentres, the retail warehouses, the retail parks and the superstores. So all of the space in central areas no longer required for shopping might be used for car parking. But who would use the car parks if all the shops had closed down and moved out of town?

The developers will have to use their wits to dream up new land uses for the central areas if the trend becomes a rush. There must be a use or two which will show a profit — but they are not easy to imagine. Sports areas, bingo halls, snooker rooms — these are all good central area uses. But developers will remember the spate of bowling alleys which were built to meet a passing fad. A fickle public soon turned its attention to other things and taught developers and leisure entrepreneurs another lesson in the ways of people.

Some developers have got together to propose new little towns or little new towns in the Green Belt to meet the various housing needs of the country — or, at least, that bit of it in the prosperous South East where house prices are high enough to show a handsome profit. Proposing bites out of the Green

Belt is a bit like stating one's intention to steal a child's lollipop. The Green Belt is the favourite lollipop of the Green Vote. No political party can afford to disregard the Green Vote. Secretaries of State for the Environment — whatever their political colour — would rather be sent to Northern Ireland than have to make decisions on the merits of proposals for little new towns in the Green Belt. Green has become an emotive colour.

It was Priestley who said 'Moral indignation is jealousy with a halo'. It is no accident that the colour green is associated with jealousy. The amount of moral indignation which is engendered among adjoining owners by a proposal to nibble at the Green Belt is in direct proportion to the amount being paid to the landowner by the developer. It is a sad fact that hundreds of acres of developable land on the fringes of towns have been labelled 'agricultural' by some planner's pen. Many of these acres have lain fallow for as long as living memory or housed some lonley and disconsolate goat whose purpose in life is uncertain even to the goat — although there is, it has to be said, a trend towards goat products among some of the more extreme dropouts. Other acres are used for the storage of rusty machinery which will never reap, mow, plough or disc harrow ever again. But, as every developer knows, a suggestion that it should be used for the erection of a few starter homes would at once cause a public outcry and the application of adjectives such as 'monstrous' and 'outrageous' to his modest plans. It is a sad truth that half the farms in this country are a blot on the landscape — and, when he'd finished arranging for his stalwarts to pick up the litter in Trafalgar Square, Mrs Thatcher might have asked Mr Branson to send a task force to clean up the farming community. Mind you, the clean-up-the-litter idea has not been a raging success so Mr Major might now give the job to some unemployed person like Sir Geoffrey Howe.

It is not the intention of this book to confuse the budding developer but the reader will appreciate that there is a lot of confusion about. Much of it lies at the centre of things — with the government. But no one can blame the government. The central administration itself is subject to a host of influences, pressures and the finger-wagging opinions of the opposition who are delighted that they don't have the awful responsibility of decision-making on their shoulders. They never admit it but just wait until they get back into power. Their excuses for disaster will have a familiar ring about them.

Take agriculture. We are blessed — views will differ on the selection of the verb — with what is laughingly called the Common Agricultural Policy. This is a device invented by the European Economic Community to subsidise Greek hillfarmers who have even more disconsolate goats than we have. It would take too long to explain all the details. The amount of written matter on the subject of EEC Common Agricultural Policy is filling hundreds of thousands of square feet of filing space. For example, the EEC directive on the import of caramel and caramel products contains 26,911 words. When you realise that the Lord's Prayer has 56, the Ten Commandments 297 and the American Declaration of Independence 300 — the Americans were always a bit profligate — you can judge for yourselves how important the Common Agricultural Policy must be.

The effect of all this is that, in a country which has been losing farm land to development at a rate which has caused fury and heartache, we suddenly find that we still have far too much. Acres and acres of farmland are redundant. Farm buildings are no longer needed for the storage of this or that, for the rearing of pigs or as shelter for that wretched goat. Secretaries of State for Agriculture, the Environment and Employment look wise and say that alternative uses must be found. So here is an interesting challenge — to dream up an alternative use for a derelict barn miles from anywhere. It is — if one can use the expression — all grist to the developer's mill.

The latest idea for using up redundant farmland is golf-courses. Some wag who probably has a vested interest in their design and construction has said this country needs another 750 golf courses by the year 2000. In consequence, applications for planning permission are rolling into planning offices all over the country. Flying golf balls will become a bigger hazard than motor cars on the M4.

The budding entrepreneur will, by now, have realised that finding a worthwhile site is not all that easy. It is clear that there is plenty of competition out there. If there is no competition, you must look at the 'opportunity' very carefully indeed. Long-established property men with a wealth of experience have learned to be fast on their feet. Most of the developable land is zoned for something else even when it is ideal for development. So how does the developer get started? If this little book is to have the serious purpose of tuition, that question has to be faced.

It is a matter of fact that this country went through a decade of in-built obsolescence during the post-war years. From 1956 to about 1966, we enjoyed (again if that is the right word) a period of matchbox architecture built of materials and with technologies to match the quality of design. Those buildings could be refurbished. Or, better still, they could be demolished and redeveloped.

It may seem to the uninitiated that the demolition of twenty- or thirty-year-old buildings is a bit drastic when most of the country is wedded to the principle of hanging on like grim death to those which are hundreds of years old. Not a bit of it. It is all to do with simple arithmetic and inflation accounting. Just imagine a late 1950s building designed with all the imaginative flair of three Oxo cubes one above the other but with windows. It has a poor gross/net ratio — and, if you don't know what that means, ask any architect and, if he doesn't know, don't employ him because his buildings won't make you any money. Because it doesn't have air conditioning or trunking suitable for computers and all the other technologies now necessary to modern administration, the building attracts a relatively low rent. If it had all those things, a good gross/net ratio, a really prestigious marble entrance hall, large floor spaces and car parking, it would attract a much higher rent.

This is where the arithmetic comes in. A few simple sums will soon tell you if it is worth buying it, knocking it down and starting again. You will have taken into account the cost of money, the cost of building, marketing expenses, professional fees and demolition — but the sums are still fairly simple. We will do some later.

Another popular method of increasing a development portfolio is through the purchase of buildings for refurbishment. Unless they are listed, you can extend buildings upwards, sideways or any other way you think might work by about ten per cent. Linked to some tasteful refurbishment, this can produce a handsome bonus and bring your building to a size which will appeal to a wider market. But you have to be careful. Some buildings are listed as being of architectural or historical interest and planning authorities can be very touchy about extensions which tamper with elevations or interfere with roof lines, particularly if Queen Elizabeth slept there.

It would be wrong to give the impression that finding a site or other form of development opportunity is impossible. Every day, developers and others find a development opportunity. Every day, pages of the local authority planning registers are filled with applications for planning permission of varying degrees of optimism. Every week, the local authorities themselves make it known that some development opportunity is available and that they seek a development partner to exploit it. Developers — the best developers — can see opportunity everywhere. They see it in very old buildings and the not so old. They see it in vacant sites — suitable for a single house on a garden plot, on a parking lot or in that fallow pasture housing that inevitable lonely and disconsolate goat. They see it in the marriage of several buildings, the sites of which make up the base for some gigantic skyscraper which is just what the expanding companies — if any — are looking for. They see it in surplus land owned by British Rail and dream of employing long, thin architects who will design long, thin developments to match. They see it everywhere.

They hope, of course, that one of their fast-footed competitors has not also seen it six months earlier. And they also hope that, if they can get an option on the site or building, they can get planning permission. But that, of course, is quite another story.

4 GETTING PLANNING PERMISSION

Planning law and procedure in this country are regarded by the kindest among us as the most sophisticated in the world. This, at its best, is a misleading opinion. Certainly, if making more than a meal of constructing the most simple and inoffensive front porch can be called sophisticated, that is what we have. But in truth, what we also have is a jungle. Ask any developer. He will take on a choleric look, mutter darkly and then describe it in words of pure Anglo-Saxon.

The problems really began in the immediate post-war years. Our wartime experiences had shown us that statutory services such as civil defence, fire brigade and other emergency activities were best dealt with on a national or, at worst, regional basis. Before the war started, local authorities had developed a considerable insularity. Fire engines, called to the scene of a fire by an innocent member of the public unaware of the rigidity of local government boundaries, would screech to a halt just beyond squirting distance simply because to go further would cause awful complications in the rate books. There was a sordid little story about a body washed ashore exactly on the boundary between two seaside councils' areas of responsibility. Its head was in one district and its feet were in another. Local council inspectors watched the flood tides with bated breath hoping that the corpse would be floated into the other's territory. Mother Nature chose not to be co-operative. Then, someone remembered that land below the tide belonged to the Crown and the matter was referred to some obscure Whitehall Department where it probably still rests. What actually happened to the corpse is not known.

It is quite clear that wars could not be won or even lost on the basis of such an administrative shambles. Many of the wartime public services were re-formed as national organisations. When Attlee swept into power in 1945, he and many of his colleagues thought that a return to the old ways would be a backward step and everyone was all agog to witness the new dynamic progressive socialism. The National Health Service Act, the National Assistance Act, the Civil Defence Act — all of these went towards wider administrations or the counties who were given a whole new pile of powers and duties. Among this plethora of statutory whim came the Town & Country Planning Act, 1947.

We had had earlier planning legislation, of course. There was the Restriction of Ribbon Development Act way back in 1932 which was designed to prevent developers putting up buildings alongside roads which actually went somewhere. But the war had demolished large parts of our cities and the politicians — and their lackeys, the parliamentary draftsmen — decided that what was needed was a strong, forceful bundle of restrictions which really had teeth.

The 1947 Act really had a dramatic effect. It codified everything and, as a piece of draftsmanship, it was masterly. It created, virtually at a stroke, an entirely new profession — the planners. These came in all shapes and sizes from all places and professions. Nobody doubted that we needed planning but, in truth, the country and its people were ill-prepared for it. There were quite a few people about who could properly be described as planners but, generally, the breed was in short supply. Other professions — like surveyors, architects and even economists — jostled for position.

The government of the day gave itself a breathing space by declaring an appointed day when the Act was to come into operation some distance ahead in the calendar. This gave time for a spate of statutory rules and orders, for the design of forms of extravagent complexity and for the lawyers to burn the midnight oil discovering loopholes through which they and their clients could drive the proverbial coach and four. To add to the complications, the Act created development charges and a body called the Central Land Board — which nobody could properly understand and which was eventually scrapped. It has reappeared in other guises in subsequent Acts of Parliament but the British system of democratic government ensures a fairly short life for most things — even promises.

Those who had inspired it regarded the Act as a device to foster creative planning by the local planning authorities. These were to be the county councils and the county boroughs — the latter now extinct. The county councils immediately prepared delegation agreements which foisted much of the responsibility onto the districts — the same district councils which had shown such commendable insularity before the war. It has to be said that planning is a big subject demanding big minds. It required bigger minds to understand the procedures, the forms and the policy behind some of the decisions.

So that they didn't lose total control, the county councils created area committees representative of the district councils covered by the areas. They appointed area planning officers who examined all planning applications and decided whether or not permission should be given. If the district council agreed with the area planning officer, it could issue the permission document. If it didn't agree, then everyone sulked for ages until the applicant emigrated. Half the populations of Canada and Australia consist, they say, of disgruntled applicants for a UK planning permission.

The basic mistake in the Act (and the late Lord Silkin will forgive us for saying this) related to the 'Deemed Refusal'. If an application became lost in the maw of the system or if there was a disagreement between the area planning officer and the district council or if no one could make up his mind, there was a risk that it would not be determined within the period speci-fied in the Act. This allowed the applicant to appeal against the Deemed Refusal to the Secretary of State for the Environ-ment — although, in those days, he was called something far less grand. This absolved the local planning authority and the district council from the awful responsibility of actually making their minds up. If — and this is the point — the Act had said that an undetermined application should be deemed to be approved after a decent period, the effect would have been electric. Local planning authorities, district councils, area planning officers and all the rest would really have had to get their skates on. As it was, the planning process became slow and, gradually, slower. Sometimes, it ground to a total halt.

It probably wouldn't have been so bad if they had left the original Act alone. Politicians find it difficult to leave anything alone but the clever lawyers had found some loopholes, some architects developed frightening skills in maximising plot ratios and most local councillors hadn't understood the original Act anyway. The Act became an instrument of development control — the big no — instead of the creative piece of legislation it had been intended to be.

All this power in the hands of the local politicians didn't prevent the erection of some awful buildings. Long debates about a proposal to build a garage beside a semi-detached house were commonplace while some dreadful multi-storey office block apparently designed by a passing tramp slipped through on the nod. It was an interesting time. We were in the period of the matchbox functional and whether the building was intended for commercial, residential or industrial occupation seemed to make no difference. In central areas, we built tower blocks. In rural areas, we laid the tower blocks on their sides and put the doors in a different place. If a building was to be used for industrial purposes, it was still laid on its side but the floors and walls were left out to provide plenty of internal turning or manufacturing space.

It was also a critical period. Everyone was learning — the architects, the planners, the surveyors, the economists, even the councillors themselves, but they usually took longer. There were conferences, seminars, courses — all manner of things to increase understanding and efficiency. Debate was intense.

Theory came alive at the people's expense. Residential tower blocks were proved to be socially acceptable by the theorists until they were actually built and lived in.

After the abandonment of building licensing in the 1950s, everyone wanted a planning permission — particularly the developers. So far as they were concerned, such was the demand for space from businesses expanding after years of war and waiting that a planning permission was as good as printing bank notes. The big money meant the rise of developer million-aires who could make quite an impression on some lowly-paid planning officer behind the enquiries counter at the Town Hall. There was talk of corruption — valuable planning permissions being bought for money, holidays in the Bahamas or even sex. Although one or two people actually went to prison for flouting our planning system, corruption shouldn't be regarded as having any part of the process. We don't have a corrupt system in this country. What we have is politics.

It may have come to the reader's notice that certain local authorities have been labelled as militant. The militant tend-ency is not, however, confined to the extreme left. It can be found among retired colonels, bored housewives, well-meaning insurance clerks and used-car salesmen who make up the membership of the planning committees. Removed from their roses, their kitchens, their office desks or their car lots, they become militant, whatever their political label. They have occasional rows between themselves, of course, but mostly they adopt a policy of demanding from an applicant the reason why he should be allowed to do something when they should be asking themselves why he shouldn't just get on with it.

So the would-be developer is up against it from the start. Don't forget that the label 'property developer' has a nasty ring about it in most people's ears and the ears of the planning committees are no exception. An application by a developer for the refurbishment of a Queen Anne house at enormous expense to provide elegant offices will be an affront. The fact that the house is too big for use as a single dwelling and uneconomic to break up into flats will be disregarded. The fact that, failing use as offices, the place could well fall down in a year or two is ignored.

These are, of course, gross generalisations. Local planning authorities are not all the same. If they were, half the excitement would be removed and developers would probably go

into the casino business. But the general truth is a raised warning finger that the road to planning permission is neither straight nor clear. You may spend weary hours, days, weeks, years, assembling a site of significant proportions. The buildings on it may have outlived their usefulness and meet no criteria in terms of modern high tech occupation. You may search the world for an architect with a talent and the reputation to create an exceptional design. And the planning committee will turn you down. If you need confirmation, Lord Palumbo will provide it.

The truth of the matter is that local planning committees

have set themselves up as arbiters of public taste. This may sound a bit like *1984* — although George Orwell never actually went quite so far. Some local planning authorities have actually appointed directors of aesthetic design — the precise titles vary but the principle remains constant. It has been said by those who travel extensively that the cities of the world are all beginning to look alike. Great office towers rise up on both sides of wide thoroughfares and, at ground level, the fascias and displays of the same old multiples beckon the customer. It is believed by many developers that, somewhere, there is a factory cloning directors of aesthetic design by the dozen. To achieve this awful worldwide sameness, something like that must really be happening.

There was a time when a man could build his folly. He could add a turret here, a dome there, for no other reason than that he felt like it. Most of the stately homes which are now listed buildings and part of our country's rich architectural heritage have elements which would not pass the scrutiny of the director of aesthetic design. Barry, Wren and Nash would all have had just as wearisome a time as the present-day developer and his architects — not that they didn't.

There is, you might say, no justice. A proposal for a modest little building in a provincial market town can cause an absolute furore. The developer — and it might be you — will be labelled a philistine, a rapist and a capitalist thug. The government can, at the same time, carve a slice off the Dartmoor National Park for a motorway and devastate the Garden of England with all the appurtenances of a Channel Tunnel — and then close down for the summer recess so that no one knows where they all are. No, perhaps there is no justice.

So how do you get your planning permission? Well, first, you get some forms and some explanatory notes from the local Planning Office. When you have read them carefully, served any necessary notices required by the Act, drawn some plans (and even for what they laughingly call outline planning permission these days, you will probably need working drawings), you take it down to the same planning office where it will be registered. They give it a number. A bit like a lottery ticket . . !

If a local planning authority fails to give a decision on a planning application within the specified statutory period or refuses permission for stated reasons, the applicant has the right of appeal to the Secretary of State for the Environment. How you deal with this situation depends on your place in the development hierarchy. If you have not graduated above residential conversions in Shepherds Bush, you may decide that massive expenditure on procedures which can be quite complicated is unjustified. On the other hand, if you are at the top of the development tree and concerned with a multi-million pound project, the cost of the appeal itself might well pale into insignificance beside the all-in cost of the rest of your expenses.

There are two kinds of procedure — written representations and the full public local inquiry. Both start off on the same form. After that, they become quite different. Written representations take a few months of to-ing and fro-ing — say six to eight — whereas the full public local inquiry can take anything up to eighteen months or two years. The cost of written representations can be quite low — the cost of a bit of typing and a stamp or two — while the cost of a full public local inquiry can lurch into six figures, depending on its length and complexity and on the prodigality of the developer and his advisors.

Let us start at the cheap end. Let us imagine that a local authority has refused your application to convert a house into a number of flats. After all, you have to start somewhere. When permission is refused, the reasons for refusal have to be stated. Reasons for refusal depend, to a large extent, on the imagination of the planning officer who has drafted them. Although the reasons are often based on established policy and are, in consequence, meaningless to the man in the street, the planning officer occasionally sneaks in a few more for good measure. The applicant, who had no idea he was being quite so outrageous in his proposals, has to examine the reasons for refusal and produce his own counter-reasons for permission to be granted. If the applicant — who now becomes the appellant — is a determined DIY fanatic, he can carry on the written representations himself. His counter-reasons are sent to the local planning authority who then counter his counter-reasons. But don't worry. The local authority's counter-counter-reasons are then sent back to the appellant who can then pooh-pooh everything the local authority has said. In this democratic society of ours, the appellant gets the last word. All of this paper is then referred to an Inspector appointed by the Secretary of State for the Environment. The Inspector's job is to try to make sense of all this to-ing and fro-ing and make a recommendation to

the Secretary of State that the appeal should or should not be dismissed in words which the Secretary of State will understand. And this, in itself, is not all that easy.

If that sounds complicated, the full public local inquiry is a three-ring circus in comparison. It is also potentially very expensive. It all starts innocently enough in the same way with the form on which the appellant ridicules the local planning authority's reasons for refusal. If the proposed development is important enough and expensive enough, the nervousness of the developer increases in direct proportion. He consults his solicitor on the grounds of appeal. Solicitors, in important cases, have schizophrenic tendencies. They find it difficult to make up their minds. One well-known and remarkably successful developer has, for years, insisted on being served by a one-armed solicitor because he is tired of the phrase 'on the other hand'. Solicitors often recommend, because of this extraordinary condition, that the developer should seek Counsel's opinion. This adds hugely to the cost — because, in time, the Counsel will probably present the appellant's case at the public local inquiry and he will need a Junior to carry his file of precedents.

Once grounds of appeal are agreed, they are typed on the form which, of course, is sent to the local planning authority by the Secretary of State for the Environment. The Secretary of State appoints an Inspector and a date is fixed for the hearing. The date is usually next year whatever the month in which the appeal was lodged. The hearing — the public local inquiry — is conducted on the same lines as a court case. A lot of time is taken up by eminent Counsel being terribly sharp and clever — particularly in cross-examination of expert witnesses on both sides who cost almost as much as the eminent Counsel. Proofs of evidence, exhibits A to Z — even to ZZ if it is a really important case, photographs of the site from all angles, photographs of models of the development from all angles, lists of independent witnesses who, in a flash of publicity, blow a developer's dreams away — all of this is assembled in piles by the Inspector. He also makes notes in a large book in a painstaking hand.

Inspectors are normally terribly nice, homely people. After every public local inquiry, both sides are convinced that they have won — simply because the Inspector has been so nice. But it is his job to make a recommendation to the Secretary of State — just as it was in the case of written representations but anything up to £100,000 later depending on the eminence of the Counsel, his Junior, the expert witnesses and the number of days the inquiry had lasted.

What actually happens in Marsham Street (where both the Secretary of State and the Planning Inspectorate have their offices) when the Inspector actually makes his written report is not entirely clear. Sometimes the Secretary of State accepts the Inspector's recommendations; sometimes he does not. Some cynics — from both local planning authorities and the serried ranks of appellants — believe that there is a bare room in Marsham Street which contains only a velvet cushion on which sits a single coin — to be tossed in cases of extreme difficulty. But even the percentage rule discounts that theory.

There was a time when the process of obtaining planning permission was fairly straightforward. It was something to be argued about between the applicant and the local planning authority. In the early days, the planners had not had the time to prepare structure plans, county plans or guidance notes. In fact, only a few of them had actually had the time to read the 1947 Act let alone understand it. So it was a straight fight built on a degree of ignorance on both sides — and most of us involved had been fighting for at least a year or two during the period up to 1947 and were accustomed to fighting real wars in total ignorance of the strategy, the tactics or why we were there in the first place.

But, then, someone — it is not terribly clear who it was — invented the idea of public consultation. It is a sad fact that the British warm to this kind of thing. Ask a Brit his opinion and you will get it. You will have seen the great British public on television asked to express a view about some pressing matter. Typically, she will be carrying her heavy shopping basket home. She will look with deep suspicion at the interviewer and she will think that the subject of the discussion is disgusting or a disgrace. It doesn't seem to matter what it is — for her, everything is reduced to being either disgusting or a disgrace.

The trouble is, that, being residents of a free country, the British public is delightfully inconsistent. The next person questioned will express the contrary view — 'Well, it's all right, innit? I mean, it's good for jobs, innit?' The third one won't know. She will hurry past convinced that she's either left the gas on or is about to be asked something very embarrassing about AIDS. So, whatever the question, the answer is one-third yes, one-third no and one-third hurrying home to turn the gas off. That's why elections in this country are such a lottery.

Public consultation in planning is, similarly, a lottery. But it is weighted heavily in favour of the anti-developer lobby.

There are several levels at which consultation takes place. At the very top of the consultation tree sits the Royal Fine Art Commission. This is the organisation which is regarded as the official custodian of good taste. Many developers, it must be said, although they realise that the Commission has to be courted, wooed and, if possible, seduced, are gravely suspicious of it. Some at least of its members are regarded as progressives — who can't be relied upon to support mock-Tudor elevations in an essentially first Elizabethan environment. And, because they look at all proposals in isolation, there is sometimes what appears to be an eccentric inconsistency in their views.

This has an unnerving effect on both the developer and his architect. Designs are prepared with one eye on the Commission — who, the day before, may have come out heavily in favour of a trendy tower block with half the scaffolding left on it as a design feature and, the day before that, have preferred, on another site, in another place, a classical form based on the Coliseum in Rome.

Vying for the leading spot in the developer's rash of acne is now English Heritage — an organisation with all the promise of mayhem in the camps of those who want to change the face of modern Britain. Its particular responsibility is the protection of historic buildings and monuments but, as you can see St Paul's

and Salisbury Cathedral from miles away, English Heritage
might just be tempted to regard the whole landscape — both
urban and rural — as its oyster.

Only a little further down the scale are the special interest
groups. Although they have no official position, they have
developed forbidding reputations as protectionists. They have
names like The Georgian Group, The Victorian Society —
even, so far as I know, The Nash Fan Club. These were set
up by well-meaning and knowledgeable people who admired a
particular style or a particular period. They are knowledgeable
about their chosen period and fiercely protective of it. They
should, therefore, fall into the category of those with vested
interests. But, because they are erudite, articulate — sometimes
even noisy — they have the ear of the local planning authority.

Below them come the community groups. They may be
residents or ratepayers' associations. They may be organisations
created *ad hoc* to object to or fight off a particular threat. They
may be archly political. Or they may just be the local young
farmers' club who think a new hotel would damage their rural
peace and want to object to it. Young farmers' clubs, themselves, sometimes develop a reputation for damaging rural
peace — particularly after the annual dinner and dance — and
hotel proprietors have been known to form their own defence
against them.

There are dozens of organisations of this kind. Chambers of
commerce, the local trades council, the town historical society,
the local archaeological group, even the local chess club — all
of these are groups of people which can get together, chat about
it, get angry about it and organise resistance to a development
proposal.

And then there is the private individual. Less organised,
perhaps, but with a point of view which he might express in a
way which disguises the heaps of vested interest behind his
objection. Some developers regard the private individual
objector as the most troublesome — and, often, the most
sinister. For all the developers know, he might have been

encouraged by some competitor dying to get his hands on the development opportunity. His apparent sweet reasonableness, his laidback logical argument, his well-expressed and telling points are the results of hours of frenzied work by teams of professionals using him as the sharp-end of a carefully orchestrated attack on a proposal.

All of this consultation starts very simply. A pink, white or blue notice — a lot depends on the weather because pink becomes blue in sunlight and white when it's raining — appears on the building or site naming the applicant and on whose behalf the application is being made and describing the proposal. The notice explains the availability of the deposited plans for examination at some distant office with opening and closing hours seemingly calculated to conflict with the convenience of anyone who might possibly want to object. The notice explains how objectors may submit their objections and the timing of them. People around the site of a development are often sent a letter by the planning officer saying much the same thing — but that rather depends on the efficiency of the local planning office and whether the planning officer remembers to do it.

What all of this adds up to, of course, is an awful lot of people who might have a point of view about a building scheme. And then there are the media — the national and local press, the national and local radio stations, the national and local television stations. The days of honest-to-god reporting seem to be over. These days, every media man or woman — particularly since Watergate and the chance of the Pulitzer prize — wants to be recognised as an investigative journalist. He or she has a point of view. Everyone has that right, of course, but if he or she happens also to be a keen member of the local birdwatching fraternity whose prime weekend venue for the lesser-spotted hedge-warbler is under threat from some development project, then the developer has a problem. Reports — in the press or on the air — have been known to have just a hint of bias to an extent where all the true facts just slip off the page or never make it into a microphone.

The result has been that wise developers have themselves taken a hand in the consultation process. They have brought in the professional communicators to persuade the public, individually and collectively, that what they, the developers, propose is the best thing since sliced bread and will bring unimagined benefits to the adjoining residents, the area, the region, the country and, not least, the lesser-spotted hedge-warbler. The only argument not thrown into the ring is the actual amount of the developer's likely profit.

This has created a whole new industry — all stemming from the idea of public consultation in planning. It was once described — rashly — as 'human engineering' — a description which no longer finds favour since the advances in genetics have thrown up a quite different interpretation and the risk of total public confusion. The barrage of information — both for and against a project — creates total confusion anyway. And the lady with her shopping basket still hurries home, bewildered, believing that she forgot to turn off the gas.

The promotion of the development project with a degree of razzmatazz has now become part of the planning system. It is expensive but, to many developers, utterly necessary. Nevertheless, the ultimate decision still rests with the local planning authority or the Secretary of State for the Environment on appeal. Let us consider these — the ultimate enemy — in more detail!

5 PLANNING BUREAUCRACY

Although in an earlier chapter there was some brief comment about local planning authorities and the role of government, bureaucracy is, in fact, so central to the development process that it must be clearly understood. The structure of responsibility is clear enough. Anyway, if it isn't, it can be picked up easily from a quick reading of the statute law, the case law, the reports on planning appeal decisions and the works of such leading authorities as Sir Desmond Heap who writes about planning and planning law while the rest of us are asleep. All of this will take only about four years of intensive study.

What is less clear is how it all actually works in practice. Settled and intended planning procedures are one thing but the true mechanics of planning are quite another. There are many influences on planning which stretch the imagination and blow the mind. And the greatest of these is politics. There should not, in any reasonable society, be a place for politics in planning. There should be good development proposals and bad — and any reasonable person might expect that someone in authority would make up the collective or corporate mind to accept or reject. It sounds pretty easy but it is not like that at all — simply because we have politics.

And, because we have to start somewhere, let us start at the top. The Town and Country Planning Act 1947 was a socialist measure — at least it was a measure introduced by a socialist government. You will remember that the 1947 Act introduced the novelty of the Central Land Board and the payment of development charges. It is important to understand the thinking behind this because it keeps popping up in political manifestos and, every so often, Her Majesty the Queen is expected to give Her Royal Assent to such measures as the Land Commission Act, the Development Land Tax Act and the Community Land Act. Then, when the colour of the government changes, Her Majesty has to give Her Royal Assent to a string of repeals which quickly undo everything that has been done before. It must make Her Majesty terribly cross because this kind of thing makes her actions look, at best, inconsistent.

The reason for the changes in law when governments change is that no one can satisfactorily resolve the problem of betterment. Now betterment is a concept which we must all try very hard to understand because it has a nasty habit of refusing to lie down. Betterment is the planning radish — it repeats itself regularly. It is based on the principle that, as society creates the demand for buildings, society itself should benefit from development activity. Society is represented by local planning authorities and, if one of them decides that a particular town or village actually needs a forty-storey office block, it is society's decision that enhances the land values. So society should be the beneficiary. You can imagine the kind of bureaucratic mayhem a philosophy like this can cause. First, there has to be an army of assessors to determine the values and levy the charges. Then, there has to be an army of collectors to persuade the developers to pay the levies — and it has to be said that there is a marked degree of reluctance among developers to pay anything to anybody. So the developers recruit an army of valuers and lawyers to argue the case against yet another army of state valuers and lawyers — all before tribunals specially created for the purpose and staffed by yet another army of civil servants.

Society itself doesn't seem to get much out of it except higher employment of the wrong kind. But there are strong philosophical arguments in favour of some kind of betterment levy which appeal to the Left. The arguments are sensible enough even to appeal to some of the Right. However, the idea of social benefit arising from development activity usually appeals to the Left for the wrong reasons. They forget the philosophy — and, in fact, they don't properly understand it. What is good about betterment is that it can be used to clobber the property developers who can always be set up as Aunt Sallys. The fact that the levy doesn't clobber the property developers at all because they never actually get around to paying it is not the point. The idea of a levy looks jolly good in the party manifesto. It has an immediate appeal to the have-nots who don't understand a word of it but think the haves should share it anyway.

On the other hand, although the Right generally looks upon betterment as an interesting debating point, the idea of a betterment levy strikes them as extremely socialist and therefore not to be countenanced. We therefore have betterment ping-pong. While a Conservative government is in power, researchers are feeding the policy committees in Transport House with good reasons for re-introducing the idea when next the Labour Party has the opportunity. If it does, the researchers will be feeding the Conservative Party policy committees with good reasons for abandoning it the next time around. The centre parties are unlikely to have a point of view which can actually be written down as a policy.

Betterment is only the tip of the policy iceberg. The Green Belt, the form of retailing, the inner cities, high-rise residential building, roads, bridges and tunnels — all of these things either are or can be made into highly emotive subjects. Politicians can wax rhetorical on either side of any or all of these potential arguments at the drop of a rosette. Whole forests are pulped to record the words of wisdom or folly uttered and written on these volatile and usually totally misunderstood subjects.

Unlike Russia, this country has confrontation politics where the Opposition is bound to accuse the Government of the day of being wrong. It is usually the national politicians who monopolise the airspace or the column inches — although people like Derek Hatton of Liverpool break into the news from time to time with mind-bending attitudes. In a non-racist sense, everything but everything is black and white. There is, apparently, no political consensus — no centre ground — and the actions of the centre parties themselves show that, even there, there is not much consensus either. So, at the top, we have swings of policy for political and economic reasons which do nothing to show or even encourage actual achievement. Betterment is one example. Housing is another; the inner cities

problem is another. Of course, these are big subjects. It is an awful truth that the same number of words, the same heat, the same accusations of incompetence and carelessness and the same confrontations can occur over the number of fish and chip shops in Grimsby.

And, of course, there is this great welter of work arising from all of this which demands a bureaucracy not only of great size but also of infinite wisdom. Somebody has to get it right and successive governments of all colours have relied on the great British civil service to do so. Let there be no doubt about it, the civil service runs the country and, at the top end and most of the way down, it is the least corrupt administration in the world. Although it has been trimmed somewhat, it is still large — and its sheer size can make it just a little cumbersome and a little slow on its feet to respond to crises, shifts in policy or the letter I wrote to it in 1974.

Some problems are weighty. Governments and opposition parties both have a tendency to want to refer the weightiest to select committees or Royal Commissions. This is a device to give everyone time to think and to create an official whipping boy if anything goes wrong in the future. Sometimes, the deliberations of the groups — and they tend to be all party — take an age to complete and, if our budding developer — and we mustn't, of course, forget him — is waiting for the results to get a planning permission settled, he is liable to become frustrated and a little impatient.

Frustration and impatience are just as likely — indeed more likely — at the lower levels of administration, the local authorities. Mrs Thatcher herself, supported by a handful of ministers who felt as she did, suffered frustation and impatience over the activities of some local authorities. She therefore swept some of them away, clipped the wings of a few more and, in doing so, showed the rest what would happen if they didn't toe the government's line. There is a limit to what she could do — although many people have a sneaking suspicion that she did not share this view. Many people believed that she would have liked to have made all the decisions at number 10 Downing Street — even down to the number of fish and chip shops in Grimsby!

Local authorities are elected democratically. The elections do not excite the electorate quite so much as the general elections do. Voting percentages are often well under fifty per cent and, in some areas, stick at about thirty per cent. There is no certainty, therefore, that whichever party is elected has a mandate from the total electorate to carry out the policies it threatens in its local manifesto. At one time, a high proportion of local councillors was independent — attached to no particular party and, on the face of it, free to act in the interests of the ratepayers. Many of them had a simple philosophy —

the best place for the ratepayers' money was in the ratepayers' own pockets. There may be a few isolated, probably rural areas where this policy still prevails — but legislation has given local authorities a lot to do and doing a lot costs money if it is to be done well.

In some areas, where local politicians possessed of extreme views have been elected, the old successful partnership between the councillors and the staff has disappeared. Decisions are taken on the strength or weakness of extremes and the elected are under the thumb of political pressure groups. It is a matter of fact that the most extreme are of the left. There are no fascist militant led local authorities for the time being — so far as I know.

Local authorities are at the centre of the planning arena and are therefore important to the developer. And, of course, they are concerned with a dozen — a hundred — other powers and responsibilities which impinge on the development process. Highways, parks, car parking, libraries, industry — all of these things and more make up the local authorities' bucketfuls of tasks with the overall purpose of creating balanced, economically successful, towns. It was not always so. In less sophisticated days, local councils collected the rubbish and worried about where to put it. They built and maintained the sewers and sewage disposal works. They emptied the cesspools in rural areas. A very long time ago, they even ran the local fire engine — but we have been through all that. The services were basic to say the least.

But international economics were to have an influence. Too many towns and cities in this country had relied too heavily on one staple industry — coal, ships and shipbuilding, steel, wool, textiles. When international markets declined, the effect was devastating. Wise local authorities — of both left and right — realised that they must spread the economic base wider. They had to attract new manufacturing industries, provide office blocks for the emerging service industries, increase leisure and shopping facilities to bring in money from a wider catchment. The best were and still are very good — again of both left and right. But the worst were belligerent and dogmatic. They sought to provide acres of council housing which, although admittedly a pressing need, denied space for anything else. They regarded developers as the dogs of the capitalist war and put up the highest bureaucratic walls to defend themselves and their supporters.

Many developers have a distinct impression that all local authorities regard them as the dogs of the capitalist war. This is just not true. There are some local authorities which can be categorised in this way — narrow, short-sighted and politically blinkered. Even they might — in their more rational moments — recognise that prosperity might just swing the electorate against them. Voters are like that — pretty fickle and just a little selfish. Perpetuation of poverty and a poor environment is the surest way to re-election. However ridiculous that may seem — it is the only shred of logic which justifies their attitudes. But most local authorities want the best for their people and are receptive to new ideas which will enhance the environment and improve prosperity.

The problem is that those commendable principles are then swamped by the planning bureaucracy. The directors of aesthetic design — those arbiters of public taste — have already been mentioned. Sometimes they are supported by panels of local architects who advise the planning committees on the design of buildings which are the subject of planning applications. As some developers prefer to build for the twenty-first century, they appoint very important and internationally renowned architects of awe-inspiring experience to design their buildings. Their plans are then frowned over by a group of locals who have specialised in council houses, front porches and extensions to the corner shop. Again — and reference has already been made to the systems of confrontation which we build into all of our development activity — we have a recipe for dispute. Admittedly, some designs by the internationally famous are breath-taking — justifying the 'cor, 'struth' reaction from councillors and advisors alike.

In those places where the proposed buildings are likely to have a national impact, the 'cor, 'struth' reaction has been expressed by the Prince of Wales on more than one occasion, although in rather more regal terms. Some architects — particularly those whose designs were criticised — might have preferred 'cor, 'struth' to the descriptions he actually used.

Taste is a funny thing. We all have it — good or bad — and we know instinctively what we like and don't like. The problem is that aesthetics in most development activity are only part of the story. Economics play an important role in determining size, location and design. And then, of course, there is the market for property to consider. Directors of aesthetic design, panels of local architects and members of local planning committees are not always in tune with development economics or the property market — and their education may take hours of patient explanation. Short of disclosing the expected profit, of course.

What has to be realised is that the decision-makers at local level are usually not developers. They probably have no idea of the developer's problems. When they leave the council chamber or committee room, they worry about domestic trivia like the rest of us do in between earning a living as grocers, used car salesmen, Avon ladies or physiotherapists. They could be bus conductors, trade union officials or, like Derek Hatton was, a local government officer from the authority next door. Whatever they are, they will usually look on the developer with grave suspicion. They will have absorbed the propaganda that developers are hedonists with flamboyant lifestyles bent on profit. They will not know that some developments make a loss for the first five years. They will not understand about yields or interest rates on borrowings for risk buildings. Because — as the introduction was at pains to point out — it all looks far too easy. There is always an assumption of enormous profit which can be tapped for a range of much needed civic facilities.

Another factor about local authorities is that they are liable to change their colour, their members, their chairmen and the composition of their committees all too frequently. There is one well-known development — now thankfully approved — which took eight years and three changes of political colour to negotiate. The developer showed a remarkable doggedness to sustain his interest in the scheme and, to the world at large, showed almost extravagant patience. In the privacy of his room, his charm oozed away and his expressed views on planning committees caused frequent discoloration of the wallpaper. He allegedly wore out three expensive executive toys — the property developer's rosary.

The moral of this story is, of course, that developers should take careful note of election timetables and conduct their own straw polls about the risk of potential change. They should try to complete negotiations before polling day — and spend a few hours in prayer that the successful party won't overthrow hard won agreements. The developer is, usually, on a hiding to nothing because change can come about even without elections.

The developer can, however, take reassurance that, whatever the tribulations of the system may be, it is in general terms free from corruption. There have been well-publicised examples of corruption over the years but that is humanity for you. Basically, the planning system is honest — frustratingly, infuriatingly honest. But this is not to say that influence is not brought to bear. The old boy network is strong — and it works just as well in a provincial town as it does in the city of London.

The wise developer — particularly if he is just starting off on his road to fortune or bankruptcy — will play with a straight bat. And this applies to all of those other parts of the system with which he has to negotiate. With the chief fire officer who has to issue a certificate to the effect that he is satisfied with the means of escape; with the highways engineer who has to approve the design of access, the car parking provision and the turning areas; with the building regulations officer who must determine that the building meets modern standards and is likely to stay up; and, if it is a retail development, with the environmental health officer who has strong views on such things as lavatories *per capita*, ventilated lobbies and hot water over the handbasins.

It is all very confusing but nothing like as confusing as finding the money.

6 FUNDING

Property finance should be a fairly simple subject. On the face of it, all you have to do is to buy a site, build something on it and sell the completed building at a reasonable profit. That is still basically true of residential development. Even that is complicated by market research, the cost of borrowed money, marketing, cash flows and would-be buyers who can't make up their minds about whether they want puce or purple wallpaper. But it is in the field of commercial development that property finance takes a really nasty turn. Pythagoras himself would feel insecure in the present market-place. If the would-be developer has stayed the course so far, the funding jump could unseat him.

Historically, developers once actually used their own money. Not any more. Such is the escalation of land values and the cost of building that any commercial development worthy of the name is going to cost an arm and a leg. The developer has to try to make sure that they are not his. The complexity starts with the principle that cost has nothing whatsoever to do with value. What matters is the yield which the buyer — usually an investing institution — is prepared to accept on his investment. Acceptable yields go up and down depending on market conditions.

When a would-be developer does his sums, he will expect to start with the cost of the land. Wrong! He should actually start at the other end with what any normal person would regard as the answer. If the answer is a seven per cent yield on an office building of fifty thousand square feet let at a rent of £20 per square foot (which, if you are quick, you will know brings in a flat £1 million pounds year), you will create an investment value of £14,285,714. Goodness gracious, you say, it's money for old rope. Well, not exactly. To achieve a rent of £20 per square foot outside the City of London, the building has to be something special. Italian marble in the lobby, carpets on the floor and some fairly expensive engineering to meet modern

requirements. It could take all of £200 per square foot to put together. That is £10 million — leaving £4,287,714. A building of fifty thousand square feet might take two years to build — and, if you have borrowed the £10 million even at fifteen per cent per annum (which is modest) and if you have carefully staged your borrowings, you have still got rid of about £2 million. You are now down to £2,285,714. The professional team of architect, engineer, quantity surveyor, project manager, lawyer and accountant will remove about fifteen per cent of the development cost at a minimum — another £1.5 million. You are down to £785,714 and you haven't actually bought the site yet. But don't worry. You can still buy land at £1 million per acre. You don't need an acre for a fifty thousand square feet building anyway so long as it's high enough — although the piling might cost a little more.

So you buy one-third of an acre to allow for a little on-site parking — that is, say, another £334,000 plus agents' fees for negotiating the purchase on your behalf, which takes the cost up to £342,350. You are now down to £443,364 but you have also borrowed the money for the land. Of course, you bought the land some time ago while you negotiated your planning permission so you will be paying interest on the £342,350 for, say, three years, again at fifteen per cent which is still modest. That works out at £154,057.50 and you are left with £289,306.50. You haven't yet paid the lawyer for the conveyancing, the preparation of the mortgage deeds, the stamp duty or the time you have spent on the phone to him complaining about the cost of lawyers and other professional services.

And now, so that you can be sure that the investing institution will actually buy it, you have to pre-let it. Letting fees will be ten per cent or so of the first year's rent. That, if you remember, was a flat million pounds — so that's another £100,000. It has become traditional for developers to bear the cost of the brochure, the advertising, some kind of thrash for the cutting of the first sod, a contribution towards the contractors' expenses at topping out and, of course, an expensive opening ceremony with some political, sporting or television personality in attendance to attract people to it. We are down to £180,000 — give or take a pound or two — which is still not bad take-home pay for three years' work. During all this time, you have maintained an office in keeping with your position as a developer. You have a secretary and a phone in the car — yes, a car, and that's £4000 a year for three years. Then there's the tea lady — and the lunch with the planning officer. You are lucky if you take home as much as your secretary — and who is going to pay your psychiatrist?

All of this is, of course, a simplistic view. It is depressing enough expressed as simple housekeeping. But, in truth, the financing of development is becoming exceedingly complicated and there are those among us who are apparently determined to make it more so.

It is partly to do, these days, with the sheer scale of development projects. It also has a lot to do with a new kind of developer — the trading developer. There was a time when property — good old bricks and mortar, concrete and glass — was a well-known hedge against inflation. Some people never believed that it was a hedge because no one had lived long enough to prove it but it was a generally-held view. Now, it is said, people are sick to death of being cheated by governments and prefer their assets to be liquid. That is why paper — in the form of stocks and shares — is traded throughout the world down telephone lines. It is all very instant and inflation doesn't enter into it. Everyone is now getting very excited about single property trusts, unitisation, PINCs and Billingsgate — and expressions like 'non-recourse loans' (both full and partial), 'tender panels', 'aid-discounted bonds' and 'droplock' are common. The budding property entrepreneur, not surprisingly, is left at the starting gate, open-mouthed and bewildered.

It is all part of the conspiracy. What the experienced and financially inventive entrepreneurs are trying to do is to hog the show. They want to keep the competition down to the level of an occasional flat conversion in Mile End or Ilford so that they can trade in the big stuff.

Frankly, all of this is fog. There have been trusts for sale for absolutely ages and people have been able to buy shares in property owning companies, take out endowment policies with this or that insurance company and most of us have at least a distant relationship with a pension fund. We have all had the capacity to participate in property investment in one way or another for a long time. All this business about liquidity could be designed to make the budding property entrepreneur shy away from the risk.

The determined will not be put off. The commercial property market has an estimated value of 250 billion pounds — much of it well and truly tied up with owners, tenants, standard funding arrangements, management and service charges. There is plenty of dealing, buying and selling going on at modest — well, relatively modest — levels. There are plenty of opportunities at less than nine digits. The message to the budding entrepreneur is to start at the bottom. Too many have been too ambitious too quickly — borrowing short on long-term projects which are too big and which they should have left to some of the older, wiser and more successful developers with money in the bank.

Many of the successful top-flight developers — now big spenders, with yachts and villas all over the place — started in a shy, modest and unassuming way although they would rather you didn't know that. They may have had a lucky start — a small bequest from Aunt Flo or old Uncle Jack in Australia. On the other hand, they may have been estate agents, saving their pennies, waiting for just the right opportunity. They may have bought a single but sizeable house in poor condition for what they would describe as a 'good' price. The vendor would probably have thought of it as a giveaway. The sizeable house might make, say, three flats and the profit on the conversion could be the start of something big. Three or four conversions of this kind every year for two or three years — virtually as a sideline — can provide the basis of the first step towards the big deal. The steady rise of a deposit account — or its equivalent in liquid assets — is a great confidence builder. First, of course, it builds the confidence of the developer who thinks he is a hell of a chap. But, secondly — and infinitely more important — it builds the confidence of the bank manager who will finance the first step from modest residential to modest commercial.

Bank managers are the media to fortune in these early stages.

They are not particularly concerned with professional qualifications or long experience so long as the figures look right. They like the idea of sideline enterprise and it is a fact that they have helped some sideline developers on the way to the first fortune. After all, the sideline developer very often has an assured income and some assets which he can sign away in case of failure — and that has a particular appeal to the bank manager. You can imagine the average day for the budding property entrepreneur. Up from the bed, quick cup of tea, down to the Garden. Pick up the groceries and the fruit and on to the barrow until 3 o'clock. And then down to the Town Hall for some intellectual negotiations with the planning officers or a visit to the conversion job to shout at the builder or grandad or whoever is actually doing the manual labour. And then, of course, it's home to bed because it's up at four again to go down to the Garden for tomorrow's fruit and vegetables.

As you climb the developers' ladder of fame, you will find that the cost of development, the level of investment — either yours or somebody else's — becomes dramatically higher. On the first rung, a modest conversion of a single house into two flats might still be achieved for five figures with a profit of five figures too — although the first digits are at the extremes of the spectrum. The next rung runs you into the lower six figure sums and the next rung into the higher. If you have done your sums properly, the profit will be handsome. At the top, the figures might leave you breathless. There are developers today who regularly trade in nine figure sums and one or two have reached the equivalent of the ton — ten digits representing the cost of a scheme. If they are right, they are brilliantly, happily right. If they are wrong, it doesn't bear thinking about.

The message is transparently clear. Don't rush it. As the bank balance and the experience grow, there will be time enough to study the methods of the big league; time enough to mature to the size of project which will demand the involvement of major funds. In fact, many developers do not mature beyond the simple residential conversion job. Of course, as they gather experience and riches, they increase their programmes and their progress to real fortune. But they do it by repetition rather than a gigantic step to higher things. They know that the next step up the development ladder is akin to the ascent of Everest after only ever tackling the North Downs on a Sunday after lunch. But, if that is where you want to go, be assured that there will be help. There are Sherpas to share the loads and to drag you up by your bootstraps. They call them the professionals.

7 THE PROFESSIONAL TEAM

For very many years, the leader of the professional team in the construction industry was the architect. With him was a group of experts such as structural engineers, services engineers and quantity surveyors who did all the sums, made sure that the building was buildable and would stay up and worked out how the light came on when you flicked a switch. It is important to understand the make-up of the professional team, its purpose and its aspirations.

ARCHITECTS

These are often depicted as long-haired and tweedy although, in fact, many of them are very smart, wear expensive suits and can be seen in the best restaurants. Their training is long and rigorous and the examination standards of the Royal Institute of British Architects are a monstrous hurdle. They are a mix of technologist and artist and many worry deeply about the environment, urban regeneration and the social impact of the buildings they have designed. They have a difficult job. Their technology must stretch to an understanding of a client's needs — even to the extent of working out what space he will need for his business over the next two decades. This is necessary because, as every architect will tell you, the average client is unsure of his needs, present or future. The average client has no idea what design he wants; sometimes, he doesn't even know where he wants it.

The architect has to be planner, negotiator, designer and wet nurse. The creation of a buildable design — acceptable to both client and local planning authority — is a masterpiece of imagination and technology. He (or she, as there are many excellent ladies in the profession) will sweat over his drawing board (the ladies gently glowing of course) to produce solutions to a dozen problems — problems of loadbearing, light, circulation, service cores, you name it and he will sweat. And when

he is satisfied, the quantity surveyor will tell him that it will cost too much, the structural engineer will tell him that it won't stand up and the contractor will ultimately tell him he can't build it. The services engineer doesn't seem to enter into the discussion because he is usually worrying about all the bits he had over from the last sophisticated installation and wondering where they should have gone.

In the last decade or so, the traditional role of the architect as leader of the team has been challenged. This has, in part at least, been the client's fault. The client has become very sensitive about cost — cost of building, costs in use, cost of borrowing and the cost of the architect changing his mind.

After all, that is the client's privilege. And the other professions in the team have, to some extent, tried to usurp the leader. The revolution has by no means been complete. In many cases, the architect still leads — although it is perhaps pertinent to wonder why. At least seventy-five per cent of his or her training is concerned with design and the rest with cost and management, give or take a percentage or two to cover things like tea breaks. How, ask his critics, with this preoccupation with the aesthetics of building design, can he possibly manage a team of hard-nosed professionals, handle a near recalcitrant contractor and actually organise everyone to put a complex thing like a building together. This view has been the launching pad for an onslaught on the leadership position and the creation of a new profession — the project manager — which, they say, can be drawn from any one of five or six professions. What matters in project management is personality and natural leadership — natural leadership, not the traditional I-got-here-first kind to which the team had always been accustomed.

The onslaught, in fact, has only nibbled at the edges. This is because clients, when they think of building anything bigger than a shed, think of an architect first. He is called in and he then recommends the rest of the professional team to his employer. This gift of work puts the architect in a strong position even though he may be the most inept leader and the least competent manager of the job in hand. Yes — and even though he may be scared stiff of the contractor.

To their faces, architects still command enormous respect from their fellow professionals and are sent Christmas cards, invited to golf days and taken to lunch to discuss particular problems. This is bound up with the fact that the client usually goes to the architect first. Behind the architects' backs, it is often quite another story.

Of course, there are architects and architects — there always were. Some of them somehow managed to get things terribly wrong — and then their buildings won some commendation. Others, castigated by the critics and the public generally, created buildings in which it was a delight to work or just sit. There is an extract from the memoirs of a Renaissance pope, Aeneas Sylvius, Piccolimini Pious II which bears repetition.

The Pope had received many nominations against the architect; that he had cheated; that he had lied; that he had blundered in the construction; that he had spent more than fifty thousand ducats when his estimate had been eighteen thousand. The law of the Ephesians, according to Vitruvius, would have obliged him to make up the difference. He was a Florentine named Bernardo, hateful to the Sienese from his mere nationality. In his absence, everyone abused him. Pious, when he had inspected the work and examined everything, sent for the man. When he arrived after a few days in some apprehension, since he knew that many charges had been brought against him, Pious said 'You did well, Bernardo, in lying to us about the expense involved in the work. If you had told the truth, you could never have induced us to spend so much money and neither this splendid palace nor this church, the finest in all Italy, would now be standing. Your deceit has built these glorious structures which are praised by all except a few who are consumed with envy. We thank you and think you deserve a special honour among all the architects of our time' — and he ordered full pay to be given to him and, in addition, a present of one hundred ducats and a scarlet robe. He bestowed on his son the grace he asked and charged him with the new commission. Bernardo, when he heard the Pope's words, burst into tears of joy.

These days, of course, there is rigid cost control and sophisticated computer technology to assist the architect and his fellow professionals to keep within cost limits. Few present-day developers would adopt the Pope's beneficence if the cost of buildings rose by two hundred per cent and, where costs have soared for one reason or another, heads have rolled, writs have been issued and the architect's professional indemnity insurers have loaded the premium to unaffordable levels.

As with many intellectual or creative callings, architects tend to disagree with other architects rather more than is reasonable. Half of the members of the Royal Institute of British Architects think the Lloyds Building is a modern sculpture of brilliant conception and design. The other half think it looks like a misplaced oil rig. The RIBA tends to have palace revolutions every four or five years for much the same reason.

As a budding developer, you have to know about architects. You have to know how to instruct them and you have to be sure that they understand your instructions. One eminent architect was once heard to say that, before he designed a building, he stood on the site and listened to the music of the architecture around him. If you are a developer, this is the kind of remark that should send up the Very lights, the warning cones, to signal that something might be terribly wrong. The developer has to produce the architect's brief.

The trouble is that producing an architect's brief usually needs the help of an architect. You can lay down all sorts of parameters — maximum cost, approximate minimum size, whether the building needs dealing floors (to attract Big Bang tenants), whether the offices should be cellular or open plan, whether it should be air conditioned. The best architects work up the brief with you. Some of them even work with management consultants to determine an owner-occupier's needs for the next decade or two — for expansion, new products or just space for a snooker room in the directors' suite. It can be a long and painstaking process to produce an architect's brief but it is important to get it right — and the developer has to work at it. Without it, some of the preliminary work can be abortive and expensive.

Some developers who are lucky enough to own central and nationally sensitive sites resort to the architectural competition. This is a device used by some who either have no clear idea of what they want or haven't the nerve to ask for it. Winning competitions is very satisfying for architects but winning entries are not always built. Some winning entries — when they are displayed at the Royal Academy — have viewers wondering what they are supposed to be and even some of the experts express astonishment at what is regarded as the best.

The early 1990s is what is known as market-led. As has already been said, people have higher aspirations these days. They want the best in which to live, work and play. Buildings, if they are to let on the market for a high rent, have to be well-designed to suit market needs. They have to be finished with the right materials — with a fountain in the lobby cascading over the marble. Matchbox functional was for the 1950s and 1960s. What we have now is style — and the best architects have it too.

But style in the design and construction of buildings — just as in the cutting and sewing of a Savile Row suit — can be expensive. So the British have another profession to warn the client about the excesses of the architect and to point out where the costs are going. This is the quantity surveyor.

QUANTITY SURVEYORS

Quantity surveyors are a peculiarly British invention which grew, allegedly, because architects either couldn't count bricks or just couldn't be bothered. Wherever the Empire stretched, so quantity surveying followed the flag. As a profession, quantity surveyors don't exist in America, Japan or anywhere really foreign like France or Greece. This is not to say that the arts and crafts of the quantity surveyor are not practised in these places. British developers, unaccustomed to making development decisions without the support of a full array of British professionals, expected British type service wherever they saw development opportunity. In consequence, there are British firms of quantity surveyors in Boston — just as there are British estate agents in Tokyo. Quantity surveyors now like to be called cost consultants because, indeed, that is what they are.

To be effective, they have to understand the components of construction — not just the finished structure but the labour, materials, plant and machinery that actually put the whole thing together. They have views on the materials to be specified, the right form of the contract documents, and even the list of contractors to be invited to tender. They have to measure the quantities of labour and materials for interim valuations which keep the contractor solvent and they have to work out the final account when the job is done, a function which usually makes the contractor insolvent. Like the architect, the quantity surveyor is threatened — but he is also threatening. As one who threatens, the quantity surveyor, in his role as cost consultant, has a particular relationship with the client. Some clients use cost consultants to develop the architect's brief, determining strict cost parameters which put the architect into a creative strait-jacket. Of course, if he was called in to advise a client in this way, the quantity surveyor often found himself in a position to 'recommend' an architect. This was role reversal of an extreme kind and architects who were so appointed were often very petulant indeed.

And then some quantity surveyors persuaded some clients that they — as money managers — were the best people to manage the whole project. Some got themselves involved in funding projects and were able to offer clients a total service short of actual design and engineering. The labels of project managers, construction managers and cost consultants were nailed firmly to the quantity surveyor's masthead. Some knew more about taxation and capital allowances than most of the property accountants and lawyers so those labels were nailed to the masthead too. And some even took a shy at the valuers — particularly in the field of insurance valuation where future rather than historic costs mattered most. It was all good for blurring the edges of traditional professional responsibility.

But the quantity surveyors were themselves a threatened species too. The rise of internationalism bode ill. American and Japanese conglomerates which had never heard of quantity surveyors or bills of quantities wanted buildings put up quickly for fixed prices and on preconceived designs. Some of them appointed engineers to project manage fast-track building projects without a brick being counted or a labourer's hour being measured. Whereas there had been interesting skills at the lower levels of the quantity surveying profession — like workers-up and takers-off — new methods and computer technology weeded these out. The British Property Federation — the trades union of the development fraternity — introduced its own ideas of how the contract procedure should work and made it clear that traditional quantity surveying wasn't on the shopping list.

And Mrs Thatcher didn't help very much either. Many quantity surveyors had relied heavily on local authority housing for their bread and butter — as had, indeed, all the professionals. Local authority contracts diminished — and with them some of the bread and butter. Diversification and even emigration was the cry. The net result is increasing claims to leadership of the team, direct and close relationships with the client and the right to project manage — giving everybody else the runaround on the principle that money talks.

But these are the more sophisticated functions of the quantity surveyor. What the developer wants to know is how much a particular architect's design is going to cost him. The quantity surveyor can usually tell him. As has been said, he reads the plans and specifications. He does this rather well because he has been trained to do so. He measures from the drawings the quantities of labour and materials necessary to build the architect's dream. He adds in all kinds of things that have to happen on site before building starts — and he puts in provisional sums for elements of the building which will be supplied from external sources.

While he does all this, his little old mind is working away. He might spot a design element which is, in his view, unnecessarily expensive. He might notice that the bricks specified are twice as expensive as another kind of similar hue and quality he has seen used on another building. And, of course, he tells his client — sometimes after pointing out these sins to the architect who might or might not agree with him.

This cheese-paring function — and don't, whatever you do, look upon it as unimportant — has grown into a new science. It is called 'value engineering'. It has to be said that, in creating the architect's brief, some development clients have some grandiose ideas. When the designs are produced and priced, the client has a heart-stopping shock. Although the design meets the brief to the letter, the estimated cost is stratospherically wrong and not at all what the developer thought it would be or could afford. Don't forget that cost doesn't have a lot to do with value. The market dictates value — but the hard facts of life dictate cost.

So this is where value engineering comes in. It is essentially a team exercise although it is usually cost led. Certainly, cost reduction is one of the objectives — but the prime purpose is to create a building which represents true value for money. The developer — whether he is speculating or developing for his own occupation — expresses size, function and location — and the professional team starts taking the architect's design to pieces, shifting this, moving that, improving gross/net ratios, altering specifications and, generally, cutting the architect, although not necessarily the building, down to size. The price of one building for an American client dropped from £22 million to £16 million after it had been value engineered without significant change in its external appearance or its internal functional efficiency.

The whole idea of value engineering is relatively new although most quantity surveyors will say that they have always done it as part of normal service. As a new kind of cost-cutting service, it was invented and practised on mainland Europe and in the United States — but, of course, these are the very places where quantity surveying the British way is not practised. But some British firms have cottoned on to the idea as a re-expression of the kind of essential service that they can give —

and the way costs are going, it is likely to be of growing importance.

ENGINEERS

The engineers come in all sorts of guises — civil, structural, services and a few others which are so specialist no one understands them anyway. The engineers are the clever ones who calculate stresses per cubic foot — and they will always know the real scientific reason why a building should not have fallen down. Civil engineers don't very often get involved in buildings of modest size although it has to be said that some of the structures currently on the drawing board are so large that some civil engineering involvement is almost a certainty. The professional team is likely to include a structural engineer and, in these days of air-conditioning and controlled climates, high-speed lifts and under-floor technology, a services engineer — sometimes even two. It is easy to say that technology is overtaking human capacity to install it. It is nevertheless true that client confidence is sometimes strained by the occasional design disaster.

It was a tradition that the professions were self-contained in their own little firms. If an architect was instructed to design a building, he might have to cross a whole county to see the other professions such as the services engineers. This practice was not conducive to getting things right first time. Afterthoughts such as services ducts appeared like blisters on working drawings — sometimes even after work had started. That is not the reason why the Lloyds building looks like it does. It was planned to look like that and it should not be thought that all that external plumbing arose because of the afterthoughts of the services engineer. But, in some buildings, it happens.

There is a string of examples. An architect, besotted by the idea of creating a gigantic atrium in a major building, forgot to pass details of his dream to the services engineer. When the equivalent of a sizeable equatorial rain forest was moved into the building, it produced so much nitrogen that it made a nonsense of all of the calculations done by the services engineers

and on which the services installation had been based. In consequence, the air conditioning developed a number of serious faults and, on cold days, the climate control systems boiled the goldfish in the ornamental pond. The pond itself, designed as an important architectural feature, gave off so much steam that the whole atrium was wreathed in fog for most of the day. The pedestrian flow was heavy and the security guards — now an essential ingredient of any major building — spent most of their days rescuing drowning customers.

The co-ordination of all elements of design became a matter of real concern. Some progressive practices saw the benefits of multi-disciplinary service — planners, architects, engineers of all kinds, landscape and interior designers, even quantity surveyors, all working together and shouting questions at each other across their drawing boards or desks for advice about where to put this bit or that. It was an exciting concept. Everything was designed in a co-ordinated way and economies of scale, not to mention proximity, could have saved clients much blood, sweat and cost. But only a handful of serious multi-disciplinary practices exists — and dear old professional insularity is as strong as ever despite the fact that some of the edges are becoming slightly blurred.

PROJECT MANAGERS

This is a relatively new breed of professional and the academic world has been quick to realise his potential by creating degree and diploma courses in the subject. In truth, the project manager has to be supra-professional. He has to be a born leader, arbiter, all-knowing and, preferably, a Black Belt 7th Dan. He must be prepared to go through his working life unloved.

One of the problems about this profession is the wide range of definitions of the job itself. What is project management to one is construction management to another and something quite different to somebody else. The surveyor in general practice — who also claims a right of leadership and the project management function — might include funding and disposal in the job specification whereas an architect-cum-project manager would never dream of it. It is a function in transition and only time will tell us what the job really should be.

THE LETTING AGENT

Let us call him that for the moment. It is his responsibility to dispose of the building — first, to let it to a tenant or tenants and, secondly, perhaps to sell the completed and let building to an investor. This is a pure agency function with a bit of marketing thrown in. In fact, the letting agent has an important part to play in the creation of the building, its location, its floor sizes and its performance standards. He will know what the market will stand in terms of rent, what yield the building will show and therefore the ultimate sale price to a financial institution. He has a decisive role — because his opinion will determine land values, building cost parameters and facilities.

He is usually a cheerful pessimist. A few words from him and the developer client will want to take up plate decoration. His opinion often consists of a jumble of incompatibilities because he will demand the highest standards (which means the highest cost) to achieve the minimum rent. He will point to a dozen sites in the area better than the one available for reasons of communication, facilities and the absence of mosquitoes. But he mustn't be ignored. He is helping to mould the product to suit his perception of the market — an essential part of the marketing mix.

It has to be said that the commercial letting agent is usually far more than that. He (or she) is usually a chartered surveyor, a title bestowed on him — or her — after grinding through examinations as stringent as any professional examinations can be. Chartered surveyors come in many guises but those in general practice cover a wide range of activities. They can, for example, be concerned with investment, advising pension funds and insurance companies on opportunities worth millions — no, billions — of pounds. But, to the developer, their value lies in their knowledge of the market-place — the needs of the consumers of all this real estate that is being designed, being built or just lying about.

Mind you, they have their faults. They issue market reports, location reports, yields tables and the results of the most erudite research. They prognosticate about the future of retailing, the demise of high tech, the threat of the metrocentre and the need for inner-city regeneration. They don't think much of the sites you buy — particularly if you have bought them from another agent — and they write long letters and reports giving good reasons why you should not expect the rent or the price you have hoped for.

Quite apart from all that, the really clever ones have led the changes in funding over the years. They are probably behind some of the more esoteric arrangements referred to in another chapter. Almost certainly, they are behind unitisation and PINCs. And those really clever ones work for enormous practices with resources unmatched even by some of the larger development and investment organisations — resources both financial and intellectual of mind-boggling proportions.

THE LAWYER
We dealt at some length earlier with the lawyer and the planning process. In fact, such is the complexity of property and planning law that lawyers are an essential part of the professional team. They have many skills. They can find a valid objection to every possible solution. They cause developers more sleepless nights than Bo Derek and, as we have said earlier, the different elements of the legal profession unite to sap the hope from every scheme. That is, of course, until it is finished and let. They will then attend the opening ceremony, sip the champagne and begin to show real confidence in the outcome — subject to reservations, of course.

. . . AND THE REST
It would be wrong to stop the list there. There are, in fact, many more professionals with whom the developer must learn to cohabit. There are traffic engineers, for example. If your scheme is big enough, it will generate traffic. A shopping centre

will, these days, probably have a sizeable car park. It will need turning space for the massive delivery vehicles serving the shops. The highways engineers working for the local authority will lay down dozens of requirements and conditions which might — probably will — cost you the earth. The private traffic consultant is a kind of mathematician on wheels. He will produce argument and counter-argument to bewilder the local authority's highways engineer until his requirements and conditions are reduced to pulp. And, with a little bit of luck, it will have cost you marginally less than your compliance with the requirements and conditions would have cost you in the first place.

There are also private planning consultants. Not all planners work for local authorities — although many private planning consultants once did. They have therefore lived on both sides of the tracks and are generally thought of as knowing the ropes. They argue a lot between themselves and with other people. They have developed their own jargon and go on endlessly about development envelopes and plot ratios. If you can find one who is a really good talker, he or she can browbeat the director of aesthetic design into a jelly. They, like most professionals, come in several grades of quality and experience. The very best produce long reports in esoteric language which the average developer will have neither the time nor the inclination to read. But don't ignore the private planning consultant. He can act as a professional witness at the inevitable public inquiry into your appeal against the refusal of planning permission. He will not only swear that black is white — if he is good enough, he will prove it.

There has been a hint that the edges of the professions are becoming blurred. What were clearly defined functions are no longer so. The major accountancy practices which were once concerned only with doing your books have blossomed with a range of consultancy services that treads on everybody's toes. Offering development leadership on a grand scale, they orchestrate the whole procurement operations for docks, hospitals, armed forces, new towns, even whole industries, sometimes even countries. This means controlling architects, planners, cost consultants, estate agents and even arms dealers. They offer relocation services, facilities planning, management consultancy, headhunting — in fact, as all-purpose shops, they are unsurpassed.

Interior design has forced itself into the developer's ken. Space is expensive and most interior designers claim the space planning function. Modern interior design and space planning are not just a matter of fitting quarts into pint pots. It is a matter of working efficiency and also a matter of working in an environment which stimulates. Good interior design makes work into a pleasure.

And then, of course, there are the marketers, the PR men, the communicators. We will meet them later but they are all part of the professional team. And they all charge the developer fees at a level which, no matter how successful you become, you will heartily resent.

This gallery of talent — you will remember that we started with the architect some time ago — is the professional team. Creative, full of flair and ideas; cost conscious, wanting everything within cost parameters, and everything properly billed and scheduled; mathematical, with slide rules and computers, providing reassurance that buildings stay built; managing with strong dynamism and, finally, telling you that you were wrong to make the development decision in the first place for good locational, market and legal reasons.

The reality is not always like that. All the client has is a site and a rough idea of the number of square feet of office, retail or industrial space which will let at the right price and produce a reasonable profit. At that stage, he has no idea what the architect will dream up — and, in truth, neither has the architect. Our descriptions of the functions of the several members of the professional team will indicate the pressures that are likely to arise at this time. The quantity surveyors, the structural engineers and the letting agents will usually fall about hysterically at the architect's preliminary sketches. Mind you, if he has been responsible for their appointment by the client, they won't do it in front of him.

The architect, in fact, deserves some sympathy. Not only does he have to put up with all kinds of pressures from his own team and, of course, his client but he also has to deal with the local planning authority. He may even have to deal with a director of aesthetic design. Directors of aesthetic design are free from financial restraints — indeed, words like cost and profit are totally absent from their vocabularies. The architect, instructed by his esteemed client to obtain planning permission, becomes the equivalent of a push-me, pull-you, facing both ways and hating both of them.

How the architect eventually creates a design which is acceptable to the client and meets the objections of the rest of the professional team is due to sheer professional skill which derives from his or her years of rigorous training and hard-won experience. How he or she achieves that and, at the same time, appeases the local planning authority is a matter of sheer genius.

Architects have taken much of the blame for our environment. Admittedly, as one or two members of the Royal Family have mentioned, some of them have produced some strange designs. But it has to be remembered that every architect — like all artists — has a patron and what the architect produces must have pleased someone, somewhere, sometime, before his masterpiece is submitted for public approbation or otherwise. He might even have pleased a director of aesthetic design who has just as much right to his opinion as anybody else — well, almost. But no, there is no doubt that architects have a difficult job. When the building is up and occupied, the architect will be pilloried by the occupants from the chairman to the office boy for real or imagined design defects.

But, even before he reaches that soul-destroying stage, the architect has to satisfy someone else. The contractor — oh yes, the contractor . . !

8 THE CONTRACTOR

'What d'yer call this then?'

'Well, they're my working drawings . . .'

'Working drawings — you must be joking! That won't work for a start. And what's that supposed to be? No, not that — that — under the coffee stain.'

Conversations like this are common in the site hut. But, before we reach that elegant little wind-blown shack with a variety of unimagined uses, we must examine the role of the contractor and his place in the order of things. Up to now, he has hardly been mentioned. Sites have been bought, money has been raised, buildings have been designed, costs have been calculated, markets have been examined, pre-lets may even have been arranged — but no one has actually spoken to the contractor, asked his advice or sought his view on a design.

To be fair, things are changing. The British Property Federation has expressly preferred a system in which a contractor is brought in early to take responsibility for some of the detailed design. Some developers have decided to bring contractors in from Day One to give advice on buildability, materials and techniques. A new togetherness is growing — away from the old ways of confrontation and hostility.

For centuries — well, it sometimes seems as long as that — the professions in the construction industry have used a form of contract which is a recipe for dispute. On the strength of it, a whole network of tribunals, appeals procedures and unlimited piles of work for lawyers and accountants have been allowed to develop to keep the contractor in his place. It is an extraordinary situation. It is also difficult to understand why this should have happened. Contractors are the instruments of building.

It is their task to translate into reality a few lines on a plan and a few paragraphs in a specification. It has become their function to correct others' mistakes while at the same time organising labour, ensuring delivery of materials when they are needed and finishing the job on time. And all of this without dispute or disagreement — with the equable good nature for which the British building contractor is renowned throughout all parts of the country, indeed throughout the world.

Everyone knows that. Everyone who has owned a house and has sought to have it repaired, modernised or extended knows all about the contractor and his band of merry — and some not quite so merry — men.

And, of course, in addition to being the butt of the professionals, the contractors have been a butt of governments. All political parties swear to their electorates their concern for the infrastructure, their desire for better buildings and their intention to build more houses for the people. Until they are elected, of course. In power, politicians recognise the building industry as a useful economic regulator — and they apply stop-go-stop policies to it with an almost reckless abandon. One result has been the loss of thousands of skilled craftsmen who have been disenchanted (they have a pithier phrase — not a word skilled craftsmen use in the circumstances) with the industry. They have been lost to it for ever. Another result has been a string of bankruptcies among contractors when work flows dry up in the economic desert which governments have created.

None of this has had any effect whatsoever on the inherent good humour of the British contractor. His equanimity, patience and sense of urgency in the service of his clients are undiminished. His respect for the professional team and his regard for the reams of working drawings flooding from the architect are high.

He is the person most affable at site meetings. His attitude to the quantity surveyor during the process of interim valuations is friendly and helpful. Anyone with the title 'project manager' falls naturally into that close circle of friends with whom he, the contractor, will share his table and his confidences. Any contractor will tell you all of that.

In fact, contractors will be ready to tell you quite a lot of things if you happen to ask. They will not always be able to tell you why they are contractors. The computer software industry apart, building contractors usually top the league table for insolvency turning to bankruptcy. In a really bad year — like

1973/4 or 1989/90 or, worse, 1991 when their clients toppled like ninepins, contractors have been known to queue up at the courts for the appropriate forms. Even in relatively good times, contractors sometimes find work flowing sluggishly and, to keep workforces together, actually tender to make a loss. This must be true — otherwise thirty per cent variations between highest and lowest tenderers wouldn't exist. And this is allowing for the fact that the two highest tenderers are so pushed that they don't want the job anyway.

But the contractors are philosophical about all of this. They are not a bit like the farmers. Farmers complain about everything — the EEC, the government, the weather, swine fever, Chernobyl radiation, burning stubble, subsidies — and here the contractor allows himself a hollow laugh. Subsidies! If ever a business needed subsidies, it is building contracting. But, in the absence of subsidies, contractors have fallen back on the game of the claim. The budding developer should be at pains to understand the basic systems of tendering and contract procedures prevalent in the United Kingdom. It is a system designed as a series of traps set by the professionals into which both the unwary client and the unwary contractor can tumble. And claims are part of the system.

Tenders to carry out building works are submitted on a form of tender which usually allows a very short and inadequate line on which the total tender figure is to be written in both figures and words. That bit is fairly easy. What causes the work is the bill of quantities. This is a device invented by quantity surveyors to ensure that there is some element of realism in the final tender figure. The bill includes preliminaries and measured quantities of labour and materials all of which have to be individually priced by the contractor's estimators. These priced bills are then checked against the quantity surveyor's idea of what the prices should have been. This information is then used to negotiate a contract figure — almost invariably lower than the figure the contractor thought of in the first place.

The agreed contract figure, as one might expect, goes into the contract between the client and the contractor. Bear in mind that the priced bill is evidence of an agreed schedule of prices for this and that. The contractor eventually arrives on site, everyone spits on their hands and construction starts. The tender documents included a set of plans of the proposed works. On Day One, the architect turns up with an entirely different set of drawings which bear little or no relationship to

the job the contractor thought he was going to do. It would be wrong to blame the architect for this. Of course, architects do change their minds, particularly when they discover that the particular material of a stated tensile strength which has to wrap round an attractive feature hasn't actually been invented yet. But clients change their minds too. Even they can't always be blamed — and don't forget, budding entrepreneur, that you are the client. Clients are subjected to all kinds of pressures. There is the matter of planning permission hard-won by the client who may have been compelled to concede a point or two to the director of aesthetic design. You will remember him — or her. There is the matter of the quantity surveyor, the arbiter of cost, drawing attention to the all-too-lavish whim of the architect in specifying sapele and wrought-iron fitments rather than deal and plastic. There are market forces — and, my goodness, they can alter a high-tech science park into a retail warehousing complex virtually overnight. And there is public opinion. If the building is important enough, even Prince Charles might have said something about it. At the lower end of the scale, even the most innocent building can provoke extraordinary hostility. Sensitive developers — and we know just how sensitive they can be — have to take account of such things.

The point of all this is that best laid plans gang aft a-gley — and some gang a-gleyer than others. Few buildings are completed to match precisely the plans on which the original tender was based. This is where the game of the claim starts. The wise contractor keeps a notebook in which he can record the outrageous whims of both the architect and the client. In this way, he can check his information against the formal statement of variations which is prepared by the architect. Contractors achieve a kind of euphoria when they hear words such as 'We'll have to change that corner' or 'That cladding will have to come off because the colour's wrong for the site'. And they have been known to develop a trance-like quality if the client chairman's wife visits the site when the job is virtually completed. She can be guaranteed to change most things including the dimensions of the chairman's office and the proximity of his secretary's.

All of these changes have to be negotiated as 'contractors'

claims'. It is an exhilarating period for the contractor who
enjoys the thrill of the chase — in this case, the pursuit of a
profit otherwise absent from his tender figure.

Such is the importance of estimating claims that contractors
head-hunted the quantity surveyors who gave them the most
trouble and offered them higher salaries and a BMW — sometimes even a place on the Board. Some contracting firms then
developed the idea of the package deal. 'We' they said, 'will
design and build for you exactly what you want, where you
want it, for an agreed fixed price.' All of this has an enormous
appeal for the developer exhausted by temperamental architects, numerate quantity surveyors and truculent services
engineers still fretting about all the bits left over from the last
installation. The idea has even greater appeal to the
owner/occupiers who are far too busy making motor cars, beef
cubes or cherry slices to spend time orchestrating a building
project.

Contractors developed many kinds of direct services to the
client under a variety of names. Some contractors employed
their own professional teams in-house so that they had the
whole range of skills in their hods or at their fingertips,
depending on their scale of operation. Some had their own
little panels of architects, quantity surveyors and engineers
often prepared to speculate for work with the contractor.

The astute reader will have picked up the subtle changes
that are taking place within the industry. Patronage has shifted.
The determined 'design and build' contractor who once relied
heavily on the professional team to include his name on the list
of possible tenderers now has architects and quantity surveyors
sending him Christmas cards and worse. The same astute
reader will recall that, within the professional team itself, the
old traditional leadership has been challenged and everyone
wants to be 'king'. The result is that everyone is now scratching
everyone else's back in the lust for work. It is as well to

remember that the client usually signs the cheques — even though he may be using somebody else's money. It is up to him to scratch the back of the funding source while everyone else is scratching his and each other's.

This is capitalism and free enterprise at its best. Although subjected to incessant political pressures, the construction industry and the professions which serve it are not usually strongly political. In fact, they usually act conservatively, spend liberally and pray for a socialist victory so that public spending on infrastructure, housing and repairs can go through the roof. This is not a cynical view — nor have the Liberal Democrats been excluded specifically. They just didn't fit easily into the sentence.

Design and build was an aspect of contracting that caused a ruffle in the professional dovecotes. In the early days, 'package dealing' was viewed with intense suspicion. Contractors offering to design and build for clients at fixed prices made it look as though the carefully protected status quo was at risk. The quantity surveyors saw this as a grave threat — and long, learned articles were written offering dozens of reasons why the client who used this handy device for getting things done quickly could be taken for the longest and most expensive rides. The architects were none too pleased either. In fact, some architects thought that they had more to lose. Contractors could reach up to a shelf, dust off a standard shed design, add a few preliminaries to cover the site works and — bingo — we had instant factories.

Since those early days, all manner of systems have been established and most of them work. All of them have the contractor as the pivot. Nevertheless, the professionals survive. Architects still design, engineers still calculate, quantity surveyors still measure and letting agents still tell you that your building is in the wrong place and that it is too expensive. The building team still remains one big happy family. But, like every happy family, the building team has its moments of modest disagreement. Fortunately, the form of contract contains provision for disputes — indeed, they are virtually built into the system. Disputes between the signatories to the contract — the client and the contractor — leave both feeling distraught. It is the professionals who usually get excited and thoroughly enjoy themselves because, for some reason which must have been ordained at the beginning of time, they cannot be the losers. They can stand aloof and, because of their professional status, can tell both sides what is right or wrong and still receive their fees. It is not surprising that clients and

contractors have taken to drinking together in public bars where no professional would be seen dead. It is also another reason for contractors becoming their own clients.

There is no doubt that the contractors are a serious threat to the building entrepreneur. In an already overcrowded business, the biggest threat comes invariably from those who know what they are doing. Many contractors cut their development teeth on residential buildings after getting the hang of residential development from huge and lucrative local authority housing contracts in the days when these were common. Then, politicians began to talk about a property-owning democracy. Contractors picked up available land with help from willing banks and developed houses for sale. Nothing trendy, you understand — but safe, traditional, conservative housing which they discovered sold reasonably quickly. Contractors developed both houses and a taste for profit. Preoccupation with the task of landing contracts for big commercial jobs was replaced by a determination to develop big commercial jobs themselves. The larger, big-resource contractors stepped boldly into the commercial sector — and most of them made a success of it. The smaller contractors watched with awe, dipped their toes in the water and were soon paddling like mad with the best of them. It is an interesting phenomenon that few developers chose to create their own direct workforces. Some of the developers who tried to turn contractor failed miserably to achieve the same success as the contractor who had turned developer.

The reason is simple enough. Successful contractors are born with a sixth sense about building — a sixth sense which goes right down the hierarchy to the brickie who knows to a lick of mortar if a design will stay up or blow down in a strong wind. We started this chapter with a piece of seemingly fictional dialogue about working drawings. This was intended to underline the inherent instinct of the contractor or his site foremen to judge what is or is not possible on 'his' site. Make no mistake about it, it is 'his' site. His are the biggest site boards; his is the plastic sheeting which protects the passing public — and projects his image in six-feet high letters. He takes a lot of the credit and as little of the pain as is possible.

And his is the earthiest of site humour. Some years ago, a young quantity surveyor was sent to inspect some building works on an enormous housing site. So big was it that there were several quite separate contracts and several professional teams. The site resembled the aftermath of the Somme. To the young quantity surveyor, it looked deserted — and dusk was creeping up on him. He stumbled across the mud looking for his contractor — H. F. Rice Limited. He came to a large hole from which the sound of British manual labour issued — the clink of a shovel, the snatch of a song and a grunt or two followed by a spit of earth soaring to the surface. 'Hello' said the young quantity surveyor. 'Are you working for Rice?' 'Watcher think I am,' came the reply from the depths, 'a bloody coolie?'

Not all site humour is quite so innocent. A well-known housing association built some small flats in central London for occupation by people who worked unsocial hours — nurses, bus conductors and train drivers. After completion and occupation of the flats, an adjoining site was developed by someone else for commercial purposes — a large concrete structure which involved pouring concrete into frames. The quantities of concrete were carefully controlled because wet concrete is both heavy and eccentric in that it tends to have a mind of its own. The frame-fills were limited to a pour of three feet for setting. It must have been the Irish Derby, a West Indies Test Match or a clash of the local football clubs which persuaded the workforce to hurry up the process. They poured in twelve feet instead of three and disappeared in a cloud of cement dust towards their sporting meccas. Twelve feet of wet concrete is quite heavy — and the bit at the bottom sought escape from the pressure from the top. It eased out a brick or two from the wall of the newly-built flats and twelve feet of wet concrete oozed relentlessly through the hole into the flat beyond.

An unsuspecting bachelor train driver arrived home, limp and exhausted at the end of his shift, unlocked his door and pushed. It didn't open. He imagined intruders, the bailiffs — indeed everything but the truth. He found a policeman in the street below — armed with a torch. Together, they returned to unravel the mystery. The train driver had left his breakfast crockery on the draining board — and his cup, saucer and cereal bowl were now to be seen set in concrete two feet above the draining board level. The story might have stopped there but Esther Rantzen heard about it — and the train driver, the concrete and the policeman's torch achieved instant notoriety. The train driver, thanks to the contractor, also achieved luxury hotel accommodation for three weeks or so while the labour force drilled out the cement.

Contractors must also face the hazards of strikes, failure of plant, non-arrival on the due date of essential materials and too many site meetings which upset the site foreman and distract the men. He is now, it seems, to be faced with even greater hazards in the form of female operatives — whole teams of ladies to lay bricks, carry hods, mix cement, join, glaze and plumb with the best of them — all at the behest of one of those strange local authorities who prefer *Gay News* to the Public Health Acts. Sanitary arrangements on site are never exactly Ritzy and his-and-hers arrangements add just another burden to keep the contractor staring at the wall when he should be relaxing with Dallas or Jimmy Tarbuck. As a budding entrepreneur, you may ask what all this has to do with you. It is all the contractor's problem, on his plate, up to him. That is only partly true. Every delay has a bearing on your profitability. It is in your interests to help your contractor to meet his cost and time targets — just so long as you change your mind from time to time to give room for a modest and justifiable claim.

The budding developer, if he has no building experience, should get to know a contractor or two before he embarks on his chosen career. Meet them socially, play golf, bridge or bingo with them according to your tastes and encourage them to talk. You will begin an educational process that could save you millions in the long term — just so long as you don't let on that you are a budding developer.

You see, the whole business of development — successful and profitable development — is bound up with two or three fundamental requirements. One is location. It is essential that

you build your building in the right place. It is no good
building a factory where nobody wants one. It is no earthly
use building an office block when there are office blocks empty
all around the site — or if the highest rent is so low that it
would be folly to build anything at today's prices. Timing is
also important. Enough has been said so far to indicate that
the path of the developer is not exactly strewn with roses. He
may see an opportunity in 1991 which is perfect in terms of
location, cost and current demand. By the time he has negotiated his planning permission, gone out to tender, negotiated
a contract and actually managed to get his building up, it could
well be 1997. Remember Brent Cross — seventeen years, if it
was a day. Delay can change opportunity into disaster. Other
developers might have started and finished their schemes,
creating over-supply. A new business park or retail village
might have opened a mile or two away and a fickle commercial
or shopping public might have changed their allegiances totally
and slipped off never to be seen near your location again.

Timing — or pace — is therefore important. It is a fundamental truth that buildings — those great inanimate slabs of
concrete, glass and steel — actually compete with each other.
It is no good thinking they don't. They compete on timing.
They compete on size, appearance and internal layout. They
don't always compete on rent because rents are under the
influence of market forces which are, allegedly, manipulated
by the estate agents — but that can be left for a moment.
Sometimes buildings do compete on rent, of course — it just
depends how far up the Richter scale of panic the building
owner has reached.

The building fraternity can help you with your timing —
solely on the strength of buildability. Some architects have
scant regard for the word. There is one building in London
which ran two years over its contract period because it was
difficult to build — in fact, two contractors said it was quite
impossible to build. The contractor who actually tackled the
job eventually made a handsome profit — which is more than

can be said for the building owner who, by the way, was not a traditional developer. He had made the mistake of allowing the architect far too much licence to design fripperies on what resembled a wedding cake construction.

Buildability means relying on earthy pragmatism. Good architecture doesn't have to rely on exceptional, non-standard modules, special materials or totally untested forms of construction. Any good architect will tell you that. Certainly, every good builder will tell you that. A bit of pace — a bit of fast-track building method — will, at least, get your building within a year or two of the market changing for the worse.

It has to be said that — just as there are architects and architects — there are contractors and contractors. Some are very good, running international construction empires of extraordinary size. Their turnover is more than most Third World countries. Their expertise is awe-inspiring and some of them have an extraordinary range of skills — building new towns, dams, bridges, shopping centres and office blocks. They have chairmen and boards of directors who haven't been on a building site for years but they have management depth of great skill and competence. The budding developer — bent on his first modest house conversion — should not seek to interest them in his little problem. He should look to the bottom end of the contracting hierarchy for service. Between the two extremes, there is a range of contracting organisations to suit almost any need.

Most contractors have come up the hard way. They are not ex-politicians, accountants or management consultants appointed to the board to get it out of trouble or to add the right tie or tone to its Annual General Meetings of critical shareholders. The real contractors understand buildings; they understand what the client wants; they take safety seriously and they understand their workforce. Particularly the workforce — which needs a special understanding.

The average site worker — and when you, the budding developer, rise to greater heights, you will probably lose the privilege of meeting him — is worthy of study. Wear a pair of overalls or an old pair of jeans, carry a piece of wire or an unconnected power drill and just stand there in your half-completed building. You will learn the awful truth — about your architect, your contractor, your structural engineer, your quantity surveyor and, probably, yourself. After all, you are responsible for the whole wretched catastrophe. Because that is how the average site worker regards it — a wretched catastrophe.

It is difficult to find a site worker who actually believes that the building will stay up.

It is also difficult to convey the true atmosphere of a building site and the budding developer should arrange to visit as many as possible before he begins his own building programme. The first impression is one of total chaos. There are piles of this and piles of that — and piles of the same thing in widely different places which is all apparently part of the overall organisational plan. However, the next time you visit the site, everything will have been moved to different places. This happens all the time for reasons which are not clear to anyone immediately available to ask. Bits of wire stick out of screed finished walls where the plans show no heating or lighting fitting. But the overall impression is one of dust — lung-filling, throat-drying, choking dust which gets everywhere. Site workers are clothed in it — like wraiths rising from the mist. You can appreciate why there is dust when work starts on site. There is a lot of soil to dig up and, depending on the height of the building, some of the holes dug for the piles look as though they might threaten the stability of Australia. And then there is the cement, of course, and fine sand. But dustiness persists right up to the time when the very important person is about to unveil the commemorative plaque — and, there you are, with a damp cloth, rubbing it down at the last moment.

Modern floor finishes, while they are being laid, sanded and polished, are great dust creators. Impassive men in goggles and masks run large machines over and over floors — sometimes walls as well but mostly floors — until they achieve billiard table perfection without the nap. It is important work because, if one section of the floor is a fraction of a millimetre higher than another, some member of the public will trip over it and sue you for misfeasance or malfeasance and the cost of a new pair of tights.

So there are all these site workers, covered in dust, swapping their opinions about the building, their employer and the professional team. And you, the interloper, are listening in. One site worker is busily doing something to a host of wires in a duct and his face wears that dazed look of total bewilderment that comes from high technology surpassing human understanding. His attention is diverted from what is clearly a monstrous problem by another site worker bearing more wire and looking covetously at his duct.

'Watchoo after, then?'

'Well, I've got to feed this lot from this floor down to the security system in the basement.'

'What is it?'

'Well, I don't know, do I? It's blue.'

'I can see it's *blue*. Half of this lot's *blue*. Anyway, it can't go in here. There's no more room.'

'Well, it says so on the drawings.'

'On the what? You don't want to take any notice of them, mate. The services engineers drew those two years ago and the architect's changed the design three times since then.'

'I've got to put 'em somewhere, haven't I?'

'Put 'em in that one.'

'That's the foul sewer duct from the toilets. You can't put wires in there — you never know what might happen.'

'Well, I tell you, you can't put 'em in here. I could knit the Forth Bridge out of this lot.'

This kind of conversation is common enough. Invariably, the problem is resolved. Expensive professionals look at the wires and the ducts, adopt wise expressions and ponder and some compromise is reached. But you, the developer, when you overhear exchanges between site workers, justifiably lose confidence.

It has to be said that modern buildings are very complex creations. Twenty-first-century technology demands wires everywhere so that every possible work station is fed with cables for every possible machine — computer keyboards, terminals, printers, facsimile, telephones and power outlets for desk lights, dictating machines and electric coffee makers. All you wanted to build was a simple office block. Your letting agent will tell you that, these days, that just isn't enough. Modern office method demands all this stuff which services engineers have to design and hide away in ducts, underfloor pipes and work station access points. It is when you get to the sharp end — hidden in your overalls or jeans and covered in dust — that you appreciate that what is clear to the designer in the quiet of his drawing office is a fog of confusion on site.

Confusion and criticism are not confined to ducts and wires — although they are always near the top of the protest list. You will hear — or, hopefully, you will hear above the extraordinary noise levels — other site workers expressing views on the design of the building, the antecedents of the architects, the abilities of the site foreman and the marital state of the parents of the clerk of works. The experience will be educational and will do nothing for your confidence in your professional team.

There are some sinister influences bearing down on the great British site workman. The two most sinister — as one might expect — are bearing down from the Land of the Rising Sun.

The Japanese contracting industry is pursuing a policy of worldwide domination of the construction market. Japan's big six construction companies already have offices in the United Kingdom and any number of smaller Japanese firms could follow suit. There is nothing very sinister in that, you might say. After all, there are Americans, Germans, Japanese, even French — all kinds of people who lead, establish and develop companies are here already in their thousands. We're a fairly cosmopolitan lot in this country and, in any event, half the workforce on building sites is Irish.

All of that may be true but the Japanese contracting industry is not like ours. All of the big Japanese firms are part of great conglomerates. They are a mix of financial, high technology and manufacturing giants all linked with highly dangerous academics and intellectuals. In consequence, the cerebral input into construction matters is considerable. The Japanese are well advanced in their development of building site robots capable already of doing things automatically and, what is more, doing them right without being shouted at. They don't have tea breaks, time off for a smoke or frequent games of pontoon, poker or dominoes in or behind the site hut.

The British experts who have examined this development in construction robotics in Japan take it very seriously indeed.

Nevertheless, some of the other information they brought back had an even greater impact, particularly on the British building site worker. He was fairly dismissive of the robot threat — it was all a bit like Flash Gordon — and, anyway, he'd like to see the robot who could sort out all those wires in those damned ducts without blowing a gasket. No, it was all that other stuff about discipline.

Every morning, the Japanese building site workforce assembles at precisely the same time. The workforce, dressed in white overalls and statutory hard hats, does about ten minutes of exercises — knees bend, arms stretch, press-ups, touch the toes, you know the kind of thing. They are then harangued for ten minutes by the site manager who sets targets for the day, criticises yesterday's work, talks a lot about honour and threatens to disembowel himself with his theodolite if he is let down. All of this gets the adrenalin going. The teams then get together to set performance standards and everyone immediately rushes off and performs.

All of that before 8.30 a.m. It would never do here. Visit a building site in this country at 8.30 a.m. and you will find vacant, staring eyes in heads still trying to recover from yesterday. And that is the site foreman. Go farther down the line and it worsens. Quite apart from anything else, the British workman has an undisciplined attitude to dress. He and his colleagues look as though they have been attired from the reject box in the Oxfam shop. That is if they are wearing anything at all because, at the first hint of sun or the first chirrup of a swallow, off come the clothes and passers-by are treated to a display of the tattooist's art. The Japanese might have a totally different culture — but they would be unwise to give the British construction workman such a cultural shock. Any site manager would also be unwise to talk about honour and threaten the disembowelling act. He would almost certainly be taken up on it.

It will have occurred to the budding developer by now that there must be easier and less risky ways of earning a living. Perhaps, a traffic warden or street orderly might be a preferred occupation. Quite apart from the site finding, obtaining planning permission and raising the money for his enterprise, the developer has to orchestrate the activities of his professional team. Even if he decides to go down the road of design and build, he may have a quantity surveyor watchdogging the design and build contractor and the contractor's own professional team. And the watchdog will bark all too frequently when the developer is trying to watch Wimbledon or Wogan.

There is another system — construction management. This service can be a godsend to the developer determined to keep his more obvious overheads — like secretaries, offices, cleaning ladies and development surveyors — down to an absolute minimum. It can also be a godsend to the developer who prefers the quiet life and two or three days a week at Sunningdale,

Ascot or Henley to hours of meetings listening to professionals harangue each other, blame each other, or, occasionally, unduly praise each other. It is a simple system. You just tip the architect's plans at the construction manager and tell him to hand over the key to you when the job is finished on time and on budget. The title construction management, in fact, covers a number of management methods — but all of them can take most of the hassle out of the developer's day and leave him to dream up his next big deal.

But, despite all the difficulties, the developer — given the right levels of inspiration, doggedness and determination — will get his show on the road. His building — despite everything — will be rising inexorably from the ground. He will feel proud — there he is influencing a little bit of Britain — but feeling proud is not enough. The purpose is profit. To make a profit, the building has to be sold. It is best sold to an investor — one of the big funds that invests its millions in a mixed portfolio including property. To be sold for a good price, the building has to be let to a tenant with a strong covenant — which means, in broad terms and as far as can be judged by anyone these days, that the tenant will not go bust next month. So letting is important — and the sooner the better.

9 THE ART OF THE PRE-LET

An eminent surveyor from a major London practice said recently that we are in the age of the pre-let. For those who do not understand professional jargon, this means that a successful developer agrees with a tenant that the tenant will take the building when it is built. The really successful developer — you remember the chap, don't you, the chap at the dining-room table with minimal overheads — will achieve this happy state without hardly spending a penny. He will have persuaded his professional team to speculate with him on the strength of an option. Having found his tenant — or having appointed an agent with the wit to find him one — the developer can sell the whole package to an investor at a handsome profit. If the buyer is an investing institution with its own skilled staff, the chances are that the institution will appoint its own development surveyor to keep an eye on things which saves the developer yet another tranche of money.

But pre-lets don't, as they say, fall off trees. More often than not, the developer is shrieking at his agent to do something when the public relations people are planning the formal opening ceremony. The prospect of a void sends a developer into paroxysms of fear, doubt and plain panic. No amount of reassurance from the agents that it will be all right on the night will do — particularly when they have been telling him for ages that his project is in the wrong place and is too expensive. In truth, it is down to the agents. The agents will tell you what a hard, cut-throat, competitive business they are in. Don't believe a word of it. It's a club. At parties, agents cluster together like empty champagne bottles. If one of them gets an instruction, he hawks it around the others in the hope that one of them, somewhere, will have an unsuspecting tenant that the new building will suit.

In the expansionist retailing sector, the agents have hot-lines to the key traders which will create the pedestrian flow. Create a pedestrian flow and the smaller traders come bustling along pleading for space. And, by smaller traders, we don't necessarily mean Mrs Brown's tapestry shop — but the multiples who, in boom times, take standard shops in a dozen centres every year. In the industrial sector, things are not always easy. Whether it's high-tech, well-designed manufacturing space or simple distribution sheds, there is what might be called a surfeit in many parts of the country. Both the public and private sectors have built acres of industrial space in places which have little appeal anyway in a country which has largely turned against the idea of getting its hands dirty. Every day, hopeful agents — pushed into action by distraught owners — send hundreds of brochures to the top two thousand companies who, if they read them, would have little time for little else. There is an upturn in the industrial property sector. The country's manufacturing industry is taking more space — and, additionally, a host of baby firms in nursery factories could become tomorrow's giants. But most agents will tell you that shifting industrial space requires a superhuman effort — and, of course, should justify a higher fee scale.

It is in the field of office space that the greatest marketing dramas are played. In London, optimism among office developers soared because of the Big Bang — a carefully chosen title which has clouded the minds of ordinary men to an extent which made them believe that acres of space would be needed to house new financial conglomerates. The cloud is mushroom-shaped. The sinister fall-out is already apparent. Agents who expressed confidence, doubt, certainty and uncertainty in roughly equal proportions now even have doubts about their own futures. They said it will, won't, can't and must last. Developers who have put in proposals, gathered in money and gained yards of editorial space because of the sheer scale and impudence of their proposals all want pre-lets. And not just pre-lets of the odd hundred thousand square feet of space but millions of square feet of it in places which two or three years ago would have been regarded as laughable.

The budding entrepreneur need not concern himself with this area of potential worry. That, one might say, is for the canaries. He will be at home with the modest little office building, elegant, tasteful and with car parking space, suitable for the thriving professional practice in the suburbs or some middle-sized provincial town. Not for him the great towers of

Babylon with their attendant worries and doubts on a nail-biting, mind-boggling scale.

In truth, there is quite enough nail-biting at suburban and provincial levels. When you only have a one hundred pounds company, a scheme costing half a million pounds can make knees tremble just as much as one costing half a billion pounds somewhere else. Even when the entrepreneur has been through the grinding mills of the planning process, the effort of convincing the funding source, the frenzied discussions with the professional team and the beating down of the Georgian Society, he still hopes for a pre-let. He still hopes that, on the day the contractor leaves the site, the tenant will move in and, what is more, pay rent.

We have not, up to now, said much about tenants. There was a time when landlords had the whip hand. Tenants came along to plead for space, took tough leases for twenty-five years and willingly paid monstrous service charges which the landlord worked out in the privacy of his own room. All of that is history. Nowadays, tenants have a distinct edge. Some are courted with money — in the form of expenditure on a building to suit special requirements or even real crisp notes over and above mere partitioning and carpets. No longer are tenants prepared to sign leases for ever and short-run leases of three years or so are common enough. There is no organised union of tenants which has brought this about. Market conditions have forced landlords to recognise that tenants — certainly those with strong covenants — are as much a key to successful development as the planning permission or the funding source.

In fact, there is a strong school of thought that the tenant should be regarded as one of the cooks of the development cake and therefore entitled to his slice of the profit. There are examples of this kind of thing going on to an increasing extent. As developers reach for the heart pills and at the risk of making them feel worse, not all of such arrangements have been made in areas where the market is dull or dead. They have been made where the market is visibly buoyant. The developers, their agents, their funding source and everyone else involved have recognised that a tenant's profit share can be justified. It means a strong letting on completion of the building — no voids, no expensive marketing, no heart pills.

At a time when completed and, as yet, un-let buildings are not exactly sought after by hungry financial institutions, a good tenant can unlock an immediate profit for the developer. If he has to accept a lower profit to attract that good tenant, it may be in the developer's interests to do so. Arrangements such as these are, therefore, not entirely altruistic.

Tenants generally are a very mixed lot. They range from the totally desirable, downwards. The foot of the curve is very steep until it strikes rock bottom — and, at the bottom, tenants' standards keep building owners awake at nights. Really bad tenants can erode the value of a building faster than earthquakes or volcanic eruptions. The devastation they can cause is somewhere near the top of the Richter Scale. In addition, they create fat files of seemingly endless correspondence and the executive time they take is in inverse proportion to the rent they pay. The best estate agents know the worst tenants and the agents' advice is worth every penny of whatever percentage you can knock them down to.

The management of buildings retained in the entrepreneur's portfolio is a subject worthy of a whole book to itself. It is not the most glamorous of functions except in the new, throbbing, shopping centres. Here, the managers are often responsible for centre promotion which provides the excuse for a hotch-potch of events designed to attract shoppers. Events are not only seasonal — although Easter bunnies and Christmas carol concerts feature fairly prominently. Wily centre managers can fantasise by inviting Joanna Lumley to open the display of boats (that should drag the chaps in) or one of the ravishing princesses to do something simple so that the centre managers can dine out on the 'I said to Di or Fergie' stories for a month or two.

Except for the most exceptional office buildings, there is really no justification for continuing events — or indeed any events at all. Instead, the building owner often has to take the responsibility for the security of his buildings — particularly where there are multiple lettings. Security personnel need careful selection. They have a happy knack of knowing precisely on which side their bread is buttered. They know, for example, the chairmen and managing directors of all of the tenant companies — and each is acknowledged by a dutiful touch of the forelock. The building owner is rarely recognised in this way. Many building owners — anxious to show off to their friends the magnificence of their developments — have been denied access altogether. If they do manage to get in, they have been frisked, checked for bombs and told, in no uncertain terms, that no one gets in without a pass. One property owner who had been unceremoniously dumped on the pavement by a particularly stubborn and unimpressed security

man who 'had his orders' sent a signed photograph to each building's head of security with a note explaining that he was five feet two inches, fierce, rich, the employer and had actually issued the orders in the first place. Such lengths are normally unnecessary — although any owner less than five feet two inches in height should bear the idea in mind.

Every building in multiple occupation has what are known as 'common parts'. These have to be cleaned, scrubbed, mopped and dusted. The cost of all of this enterprise is borne by the tenants through service charges. Even if the building owner contrives to make a profit from his service charges, no profit is worth the responsibility of directly organising the cleaning. An army of Mrs Mops would have defeated the leadership qualities of a Montgomery of Alamein.

It is generally assumed that buildings are inanimate objects. This is not true. They squeak, groan and move in the emptiness of the night which is one of the reasons why security men seem to have white hair or no hair at all. Buildings are also accident prone, particularly when the staff has gone home. A pair of candles left burning after a power cut set off the whole sprinkler system in a building of 120,000 square feet — dampening everything including the owner's spirits.

Tenants, buildings and ownership generally are an awful responsibility. Fortunately, if you are rich enough, these responsibilities can be delegated to responsible managers. Most of the major surveying practices have management departments who know all about security men, cleaners and temperamental sprinkler valves. They will devote any amount of loving care to the buildings in their charge ensuring that they are repaired, painted, rubbed down and kept in pristine condition — for a fee, of course. The fee ranks as an element of the service charge — so don't worry about it. Just make sure that the particular manager appointed to look after your building knows who you are so you can exercise your proprietorial rights and show off when you want to.

On the other hand, if the building is in the right place, well constructed and with a good tenant possessed of a rock-steady covenant, you can sell it and join the ranks of the big trading developers who are making a name for themselves. They refuse to involve themselves in the responsibilities of on-going owner-

ship with all its cares and woes. They keep their eyes on the
main chance — the creation of buildings — which they sell at
a thumping profit. There is a lot to be said for it.

But even the big trading developers whose primary objective
is to sell on have to let their buildings in the first place. It
would be wrong to hide the fact that finding just the right
tenant and persuading him to part with a small fortune every
year for twenty-one or twenty-five years certainly is not easy.
The budding entrepreneur who reads the property pages in his
newspaper — and you should be warned that not all newspapers
have them — will be well aware that every week there are
strings of lettings reported. Some are for enormous areas of
space — and it would seem reasonable to assume that, if there
is buoyant demand, letting is just a matter of making sure that
the people who want the space know that you have some to
let.

Well, of course, it is. The problems are in the identification
of your target markets and deciding on the methods of putting
over your sales pitch. The letting or sales agents are the
traditional marketers of property. They charge about ten per
cent of the first year's rent which you, the developer, will
receive. There was a time when fee scales were standard. They
were laid down as recommended fee scales by the professional
institutions and there was agreement between letting agents
that the recommended fee scales would be charged. The
professional societies laid down lots of other things as well until
they were accused of restrictive practices. The Monopolies
Commission, as it then was, got into the act as well with
the result that there is now supposedly competition between
commercial agents on fees. In fact, they still stand at about ten
per cent. There are of course instances where reductions are
negotiated. If you think — as a building owner — that you
need a second agent, you appoint joint sole agents whereupon
the fee goes up to fifteen per cent, 7.5 per cent each for the
two agents you have appointed.

Ten per cent and fifteen per cent of the first year's rent can be a very large sum of money. If a building contains 200,000 square feet and is let at £50 per square foot in the City of London, the sole agent picks up a cool million — or the joint sole agents pick up an even cooler million and a half. It is at these levels that the agents usually agree to drop their percentages a point or two which is only reasonable — and, of course, not all buildings run to 200,000 square feet at City of London prices. A 20,000 square feet building in a county town in Essex might only be £15 per square foot or less — and that brings in only £30–40,000 according to the agreed agency arrangements. On the other hand, it might be much more difficult to let.

All of this sounds fairly straightforward. Indeed, it is — when the market is buoyant; when everyone is thinking in expansionist terms. There is, of course, another side to the coin. When recession bites, when firms are slimming down even to the point of disappearance, when investing institutions are fretful and disinterested, then letting and subsequent sale are a ghastly nightmare.

You will remember that we mentioned the agents' club. When one agent is instructed to let the unlettable, he immediately calls together all the other agents he can think of in the hope that one, at least, might have a client looking for just that piece of space. Agents have now got to the stage of actually being bored by champagne breakfasts provided at the clients' expense. Just to get his peers to look at his building, the appointed agent will urge his client to offer prizes in a lucky draw. Trips for two to Paris, New York or even Hong Kong; a vastly expensive video camera: there seems to be no limit to the range of goodies on offer. One enterprising agent is giving away — or his client is — expensive shirts to anyone who takes the trouble to visit his building. And there was talk recently of a Savile Row suit for some lucky winner. As a means of restocking the wardrobe in times of recession, a few visits, a few champagne breakfasts, a bit of luck in the draw (if luck is needed), the system shows great promise.

It is an interesting fact that agents have been doing this letting and marketing job for donkey's years and, until recently, the professional examinations completely ignored it as a subject. It was regarded as slightly vulgar and not terribly professional — although everyone admitted that, without agency fee income, most professional firms would be hard put to it to survive. The subject has now crept into the syllabuses of the professional examinations and there is also a diploma in property marketing if you follow a post-graduate course of specialist studies.

All of this is, in truth, fairly remote from reality. There is still an awful sameness about property marketing. It was and is standard practice to prepare a brochure about the building and send it to *The Times* Top 2,000 companies. The building was and is advertised in the *Estates Gazette* and *Estates Times*. Often that is where everything stopped — and stops.

It is worth looking at agency practice because the agents are an enormous influence on the development world. It is true that developers moan and groan about them — on the grounds of the size of their fees; on the grounds of their failure to let buildings in time; on the grounds that they sometimes get things wrong — but the developers still appoint them to the next job. There is a good reason for this. The agents are out there in the market-place and they pick up all kinds of opportunities. They have a nose for that kind of thing and, of course, they have been trained for it as well. Many of the agency teams are within large London or major city practices where the range and scale of professional work are considerable. Some of the large professional firms are retained to advise local authorities, major landowners, large urban estates, nationalised industries and big business generally. They know a great deal about what is going on. They pick up market knowledge; they pick up opportunity — and, if they offer an opportunity to you — the budding developer — they will expect to be appointed your sole letting agents at the standard ten per cent. If you don't appoint them, you will be breaking with tradition and, worse, you will be unlikely to be offered the next opportunity — and the next one could be the plum that you had always dreamed about. And that would never do. Birth control is all very well — but not in the development business.

It is also true that the very large firms are possessed of prodigious — and often precocious — talents. They act, for example, for strings of pension and superannuation funds any one of which might just buy your building. They know all about funding and usually have access to unlimited amounts of it. They know about City grants, property taxation and capital allowances. They even understand the planning system. They can value property for all kinds of purposes — although firms don't always agree with each other. They can project manage. They can research. In fact, the whole thing can be summed up in the words of one senior partner who admitted that, on a Monday morning, he would sit down with his colleagues, each with opportunities and expertise piled high around them, and ask 'who shall we make millionaires this week?'

So, no, we mustn't ignore the agents — not if we are ambitious. And that is why, despite the complaints, the developers, big and small, well-established and less so, don't like falling out with them. What the well-established have done, of course, is to appoint a string of surveyors to their own staff to keep the agents' noses to the marketing grindstone. The agents do have two aces up their sleeves, however. First, they are often asked by big business clients to search for and find suitable premises. Secondly, they are very friendly with all the other agents whom we could call competitors if we didn't know better. All the other agents are often asked by big business clients to search for and find suitable premises. The agents form societies or clubs on specialist property subjects at which they share experience and knowledge. The effect of all this is tantamount to a large central bucket brimful of information into which any other agent can dip. In fact, such is the interplay that one wonders why it takes so long, sometimes, to let a building.

It is all to do with pressure. You are not the only budding developer and there are hundreds of development companies all anxious to let their buildings. Agents are likely to receive instructions to let sizeable chunks of real estate every working day — and they are only human. The instruction received today is exciting and interesting — and then tomorrow's arrives. Yesterday's goes into pending and so does today's because, when tomorrow's comes in, they are both old hat. In consequence, there is a standard — a norm — of marketing practice.

And we come back to *The Times* Top 2,000 companies. Every day, janitors risk double hernias carrying sacks of discarded brochures down to the furnace or into the wastepaper area. Each brochure has cost the developer somewhere between £1 and £20 depending on size, vulgarity and method of distribution. Whole forests in Nigeria and South America are being denuded to provide pulp — thus adding to the certainty of ultimate environmental chaos. Armageddon will not be an explosion — it will simply be the earth being pushed off course by the weight of all those letting brochures.

Some sophistication is, however, creeping into the business. Research is being done — market research. Target markets are being identified and computer profiles are being drawn of likely space users. Even *The Times* Top 2,000 is now being ignored and more attention is being paid to the thousands of others who may want space but don't know where to start. It is but a small wedge that is being driven into long established practices — but it is a start. Some developers and agents have even gone so far as to appoint marketing firms to advise them — and even Saatchi and Saatchi have been recruited to lend a hand. And that, as you can imagine, could be quite another story.

10 MARKETING AND PUBLIC RELATIONS

Those who aspire to become developers on a grand scale — to assemble sites, to impose their own personalities on the buildings they create and to take the enormous financial risks involved — are not likely to be shrinking violets. Except when they are assembling monstrous sites through a multitude of tiny companies, they tend to want everyone to know about their development activities. Quite apart from the fact that publicity helps to inflate the ego, it also helps to sell or let buildings and attract further opportunity. In recent years, the entrepreneur developers have developed both buildings and a taste for publicity.

The old school — those who made names and fortunes for themselves up to about the very early 1970s — were relatively shy. At least, some of them were. Some, in a word, eschewed publicity. Of course, they got it all the same. They were the chaps who attracted the odium to the word 'developer' — but who, at the same time, gave away fortunes to worthy charitable and educational causes. Their critics hardly noticed their generosity and, if they did, regarded it as a salve to the consciences for which the developers were not given credit. It was a confusing time and it had results which were to influence the industry for another decade or so.

The period during which the greatest fortunes were made was also the period of the easiest lettings. No great effort was required to let most of what the developers built — and the letting was left largely to the commercial estate agents who, as has been said, followed basic — very basic — marketing techniques and procedures. The developers met the costs of the agents' fees, a brochure or two and an occasional advertisement. In relative terms, what was spent on marketing was tiny. In the ordinary world of the consumer, products cost dramatically more to market — but, for the developers and their agents, heavy expenditure on marketing was largely unnecessary. Only occasionally were they compelled to dig deeper than normal into their pockets — and a fairly traumatic experience it was. If a building had stuck in the market — perhaps for reasons of over-supply or simply because of a bad development decision — the cost of shifting it towards an amenable tenant was regarded by the building owner as something of an outrage.

The period of the property boom produced personalities, fortunes and news. There was good stuff here for the newspapers and a handful of specialist property writers appeared. The quality press had commercial property and residential property correspondents who produced weekly columns surrounded by modest advertising. As the market became more difficult, the advertising became less modest — and, as the weight of advertising grew, so did the number of property correspondents. The agents began to feed the correspondents with news about schemes they had let or sold or wanted to let or sell. A mention in the most influential columns would send an agent into raptures — and, of course, regular mentions could result in more instructions. The agents began to see the value of publicity — for their own and their clients' purposes.

In those early days, publicity was probably more important for the agents than for their clients. But, as the market changed, publicity became more important for everybody — for client, for agent, for contractor, for architect, for quantity surveyor — and, of course, for the buildings they were putting up. The professional societies relaxed their antiquarian restrictions on advertising and the result is a modern free-for-all where marketing, public relations, press relations — indeed the whole marketing mix — have become an integral part of the property scene. But the old ways are still remembered and heavy marketing expenditure to match the value of the developer's product is still regarded as something of an outrage. Proposals priced with more than one nought are greeted with a shocked

silence. The difference now is that everyone has learned that there might, after all, be something in this marketing thing.

It is important for the budding entrepreneur to understand the rudiments of marketing. The marketing mix is standard and can be quite easily and properly applied to the marketing of buildings and professional services — just as it can be applied to consumer products like cars, washing machines and deodorants. It starts with market research. One or two of the major professional practices apart, market research did not at one time have a very high priority in the property business. There were basic rules such as 'location, location and location' which had to be met if the building was to be let quickly — but developers expected tenants to beat a path to their door. Paths are no longer beaten to developers' doors — and the tenants now have to be identified before they can be swamped by brochures, begging letters and invitations to view. The process of identification is part of market research. It doesn't stop there, of course. When tenants or user groups have been identified, you have to discover what they want. And that is not always easy. We have already explained that clients are not always clear in what they say in their briefs and they also have a tendency to change their minds within the contract period. The same deficiencies exist among tenants. Indeed, designers and contractors know that, as soon as a tenant decides to take a building, the chances are he will want to spend a fortune on it to make it suitable for his own occupation. He will tear down walls, tear up floors and generally reorganise the place until it bears little resemblance to the original. Even then, he will not always be clear about his brief and he will change his mind several times during the job. Designers and contractors are not unhappy about this.

Market research can help to overcome the problem. Market research can even identify the tenant who will take the building so that the developer can actually build something like the tenant's ideal. At worst, market research can guide the developer towards the right size, the right floor areas and the right markets. The professional market researchers have fastened on to this relatively new entrant into their own market-place. The best are not cheap and have added yet another furrow to the developer's brow.

In fact, finding out what the tenants actually want — novel though it may be to the property world — has all kinds of advantages. There are the obvious ones like being able to let the building in a reasonable period without pouring too much money into advertising, direct mail and puffy brochures. But there are other advantages related to cost, resources and speed. If a developer can determine his market through careful research, identify a range of likely tenants at which he can target his promotion and then single out one who is interested, he can tailor-make his building. This saves money, resources and time.

Some developers — indeed some tenants — favour what is known as the 'shell' finish. This has nothing to do with the selection of paint. It is simply the creation of a building complete in all functional respects but without wall, floor, lighting and other finishes. These — and the partitioning requirements — can be provided by the developer according to the tenant's own specification. So long as the tenant can make his mind up, of course.

This is an eminently sensible approach. It is all very well completing a building to a high standard of finish so that the letting agents can wax rhetorical over the sheer classical beauty of it all. But, if everything is then ripped out at vast cost, it is wasteful of resources — wasteful of money, materials and labour. When local authorities and others responsible for housing the homeless can't scrape enough money together to bring a few houses up to modern standards, waste like this could be regarded as profligate.

The other elements of the marketing mix are advertising (including that bane of 1990s living — direct mail), public relations, press relations, design and print. All of these elements bring the budding developer into direct contact — or even confrontation — with that long-haired fraternity which makes up the creative world. The developer has to learn their little ways — and learn to be firm about their inclination to spend money like water.

Advertising has made great strides in the property world in the last twenty years. There was a time when, because chartered surveyors' own advertising code was very restrictive, the advertising they commissioned to spread the word about their clients' buildings had the appeal of an empty brown paper bag. As the restrictions were eased and as the agents became more adventurous, advertising was put in the hands of the professionals rather than the office boy. Of course, there are risks in using the true professionals. If they spend hours creating something worthwhile, they want to see it in print, on hoardings or on the telly. Their media recommendations can produce campaigns which double the cost of a building and a firm hand is needed to control their wilder excesses. It is true that some property advertising still resembles that empty brown paper bag. It is also true that the best is exciting and some of the profession's advanced thinkers have introduced the equivalent of page three girls to attract consumer attention.

There is no doubt that advertising has to be strong. The clamour in the market-place is both incessant and noisy and, if a building is to be noticed, the advertisements which proclaim it have to have the visual equivalent of a loud shout. Some modern advertisements have made even more noise than that.

Mind you, the advertising world has its critics. Some practitioners have become too clever by half and spend hours dreaming up advertisements which don't actually mention the product. They are, nevertheless, regarded by the advertising industry itself as very witty and worthy of awards and general acclaim. This kind of self-adulation tends to irritate the pants off the client who wants his product's name blazoned across the nation. For property, the rules are very simple. If you are going to shout, make sure your particular public knows exactly what you are shouting about.

The public relations and marketing men like to see themselves as the pivot of all marketing activity — if they are asked. Most agents prefer to master-mind their own campaigns and, as has been said, the standard property marketing package has caused serious waste disposal problems among the country's top two thousand companies. The package consists of a brochure, a word-processed letter (which usually means it is personally addressed to someone who retired, died or left the recipient company's service ages ago), some modest advertising and a circular to every other agent who might conceivably have a client looking for exactly the space under offer. Brochures come in varying degrees of vulgarity at the bottom of the scale — rising to dazzling designs which make any potential tenant feel that he might well be over-charged on the rent. Some brochures are a simple A4 card — others are young novels in which copywriters spend more time on adjectives than they do on verbs and punctuation or, indeed, on proof reading. Whatever they are, most of the brochures land on the desks of some bemused clerks in the top two thousand companies — and it has been established that ninety-eight per cent go straight into the waste paper basket. As the most expensive might have cost anything up to twenty pounds each, this mud-at-the-wall system can satisfy nobody.

Since the Monopolies and Mergers Commission and the Office of Fair Trading began interfering with the recommended fee scales of the professional bodies, agents are faced with the prospect of competition on fees. In fact, building owners should be — and are becoming — much more concerned with imagination in the marketing proposals themselves. This has resulted in some very strong campaigns by the agents without a professional marketing man in sight. Some people still remember, with some initial bewilderment, receiving a tin of tomato soup which turned out to be a promotion for a factory building in North London. But all is not satisfaction. Some building owners became understandably edgy when their buildings stick in the market for too long — particularly when other buildings seem to let reasonably quickly. Some have even commissioned expensive campaigns from the professional marketing outfits — and even the VAT charges are enough to turn the budding entrepreneur into a gibbering neurotic.

The name of the development is important — any marketing man will tell you that. In consequence, an unsuspecting tenant market has been faced with a battery of imaginative names which will help to sell. The steam which this brain-storming develops among the creative team is measured in saunas —

and, usually, the tenant will eventually give the place his own name anyway because it's good for his image and his ego. The fact that a creative team has suffered a communal seizure creating a trendy name which will appeal to a wide market is irrelevant.

The public relations men will seize upon any excuse for an event which will publicise the building. Sod-cutting, foundation stone laying, topping-out, completion and formal opening — all are grist to the public relations mill. It is true that events can create news, particularly if a moment's inattention to some vital detail invites the inevitable disaster. Disasters

invariably accept invitations of this kind. Local dignitaries have been known to disappear totally into wet cement. Film and television personalities have forgotten their lines and where they are. Politicians don't turn up or get involved in some scandal the day before. And dozens of guests, full of chilled champagne, have been entertained in a freezing building with no services. This combination of thoughtlessness produces results which can only be described as dire — particularly if the only working part on the site is a running tap with all of the psychological and physiological effects that a running tap can bring.

And disasters can happen to the best of us. A contractor had completed an important public building in London. It was agreed with the trustees and the commissioning department that there would be a formal handover ceremony. After all, the building was an important one. The formal handover became an 'event' — drinks, snacks, presentations and speeches. It was thought that a bit of street theatre — for which the area in which the building sits is famous — would go down rather well and add to the gaiety of the occasion. A jazz band, a Punch and Judy show, an accordionist and a juggler were hired — and Savvas, described as a human robot.

Savvas' act is brilliant — and the physical and mental control he exercises during his performance is exceptional. No one told Savvas that the Chairman of the trustees who would be accepting the formal handover of the building was also the Secretary-General of NATO. Lord Carrington carries a fairly high security rating and, in consequence, the area was littered with beady-eyed policemen on the lookout for terrorists or other lunatics. Savvas did not tell the organisers that, at a note from the jazz band which went strongly into the James Bond theme, he abandoned his robotic stiffness and started a very real simulation of Sean Connery in one of his wilder moments. He leaped athletically here and there drawing from his shoulder holster a replica Browning automatic, aiming it at the passing public. This metamorphosis and the Browning did not pass unnoticed by the beady-eyed representatives of law and order. About fourteen of the hairier and larger ones jumped on Savvas and confiscated both his person and his gun. This kind of thing tends to divert attention from the main purpose of the most carefully planned event — but it was heartily applauded by the assembled crowds who thought it was all part of the act.

Apart from occasional communication lapses of this kind, the best public relations people are competent, creative, articulate and expensive. This combination of talents means that they can dream up clever ideas, talk you into accepting them, manage them very adequately and expect you to pay for them. They are best confined in a box until needed and then kept busy so that they don't have the time to think of anything else.

The world of public relations is highly charged in more ways than one. There is no real way of telling the number of hours spent on a job and, although the monthly account doesn't say so, every client knows that he is paying for a certain amount of staring at the wall. It is the only profession which actually gets paid for time spent in the lavatory or the bath — both essentially creative periods for the PR professional.

The developer himself has a personal responsibility in the marketing and public relations process. They are not activities which can be totally delegated. The developer — as the top man in his organisation — has to make himself available for occasional exposure to the media. The budding entrepreneur as a mere beginner will hardly be troubled and he would be wise to follow the example of some of the boom barons of the 1960s and 1970s who were determined to remain shy, modest and unassuming. Those men gave no interviews and remained very private people. The uncharitable may believe that seeking after obscurity was calculated to prevent the boom barons from being diverted from the noble art of making money. But, these days, as the budding entrepreneur blossoms into flower, he must be prepared to expose himself . . . and to meet the media.

11 THE MEDIA

As we have said, there is benefit in editoral mention — be it in the press, on the air or on the screen. It is important, of course, that the publicity the budding entrepreneur enjoys is relevant to his entrepreneurial role — and not concerned with oddball appetites, tax evasion or marital disasters. Unless, of course, he is a media natural — which is to say that he is a man of excruciating charm and has a hide like a rhinoceros. There are few of those in the property industry as most of the ordinary mortals who have these qualities have become politicians.

The trouble with the media is that, since Watergate, every commentator or interviewer regards himself (or herself, of course) as an investigative journalist heading hard for that Pulitzer prize. Straightforward reporting is no longer regarded as adequate. This may be due to the circulation or ratings battles which rage between the media. The press — or certain parts of it — believes that headlines which are large and sensational sell newspapers. The 'shock, horror, scandal' syndrome is used to hide the most contrived stories which are frankly disappointing. The entrepreneur must expect similar treatment. If there is a hint of a condition on a planning application or a single letter to the planning authority from a retired colonel, the result is either 'Green Belt Land Grab' or 'Planning Battle Looms In Swindon'. It is not difficult to understand the shyness of some of the boom barons.

Success is not always good news. For one thing, it discomforts the reader who wonders why somebody else should be so lucky. For another, success in the form of riches creates an immediate assumption that, somewhere along the line, the recipient of this divine largesse has been dishonest. The first reason results in the story being spiked — unless the riches

have come from the newspaper's own bingo in which case only the front page will do. The second reason results in some frenetic digging into the past or present private life of the subject. Somebody, somewhere, will be prepared to turn over a stone for a pound or two — and, frankly, who is blameless?

If the budding entrepreneur is not to be pilloried, he has to learn to live with the media. After all, it is always possible to sue if they go too far just so long as they are wrong. Learning to live with the media has become big business for those who know about these things. There are courses on how to conduct yourself on the radio and television, how to answer press questions, how to address conferences, how to give after-dinner speeches and how to control your temper when provoked. Most of these courses are expensive and their wisdom can be distilled and dispensed in a few sentences. All you need thereafter is practice and strong nerves.

If you are on television, wear a blue shirt. Whether you are to appear on television or radio, insist on doing it live. Recordings can be edited in such a way that you can appear to be saying exactly the opposite of what you actually mean. 'I don't

think that Mrs Thatcher was the reincarnation of Attila the Hun'
can sound fairly threatening if all the words before 'Mrs' are
removed — particularly if you happen to be Geoffrey Howe or
Michael Heseltine. But these radio and television engineers are
extraordinarily clever with their buttons, switches and splices.
So do it live!

And don't lounge about on television. Keep rock steady and
always turn your best side to the camera with the red light
on — if you happen to have a best side. Noses and ears (or
any other parts for that matter) should not be picked, scratched
or in any way interfered with. Spectacles, if they are worn at
all, should be kept on or off throughout. Constant removal and
replacement cause light spots all over the screen which upsets
the engineers. Wear the lightest of summer suits even if it
means wearing a fur-lined coat to the studio. It can get very
hot under all those lights and, if you sweat, the viewing public
and the interviewer will think you are guilty of something even
if you are talking about singing madrigals in your local church.

Make up your mind about what you want to say and say it. Don't
worry about the question. It is always possible to detect the
Members of Parliament who have been on one of these courses.
They always say 'Before I answer the question, it is important
to understand . . .' They then go off into what sounds like
a prepared statement of amazing brilliance, full of statistics,
quotations and references to social trends that have no bearing
at all on the question asked. Interviewers are only human and
the chances are that he or she will become bemused and forget
the question as well. It is for that reason that interviewers
themselves are going on courses to improve concentration —
which is difficult when the producer is bellowing in your ear
all the time.

Newspaper journalists are quite a different problem. Every
month, the average national property columnist receives something like 750 press releases, 144 invitations to lunch and
roughly the same number of invitations to press conferences
and functions of one kind or another. Every property

journalist — well, nearly every property journalist — is treated in the same way. The reason for all of this activity is bound up with 'success' — a successful sale or letting, the launch of a new multi-million pound project, a turgid report on investment yields. Each property journalist knows that every other property journalist has the same stories — and a fairly boring bundle of copy they make. So what do they do? It is not our place to give away trade secrets but there are, as they say, ways.

Imagine a journalist, drumming his fingers on his desk, hoping that Centre Point will fall down so long as he gets the story first. His copy deadline for his widely-read column is staring him in the face. He has read the releases about those fish and chip shop lettings in Grimsby at undisclosed rents and not one of them has inspired him to write a word. So he rings up a developer.

'Morning, Godfrey; Bruce here.' (The names are fictitious, of course.) 'I hear they're turning down your City Road scheme.'

'Well, it's the first I've heard about it . . .'

'Really? I mean I'd have thought someone would have mentioned it . . .'

'I think it's a disgrace. I know they're not too happy with the 72-storey block but they . . .'

'What do they want then?'

'Well, they want thirty-six — and I might settle for forty because it still might be viable.'

You see how it goes. The story headline might be 'City Road Floorspace Could Be Halved' — and subtitled 'Developer Prepared To Compromise'. The journalist knows it's a good story — and he knows no other journalist will have it because there wasn't a story in the first place. This salutory little tale — which has no basis in fact — is merely a warning.

Press conferences are not the most popular form of relaxation for journalists. There are usually too many journalists about to make the trip worthwhile. They would much rather have a well-written press release and the availability of a spokesman on the other end of the telephone to answer questions which no other journalist can hear. Most journalists regard press

conferences as other people's ego trips — and journalists prefer ego trips of their own.

It would be wrong to use the threat of the media as a means of diverting the budding entrepreneur to some other gainful employment. It is a fact, so far as we know, that no property columnist has so far won a Pulitzer Prize. Property columnists, taking everything into account, are a fairly friendly lot who have dogs and dig the garden at weekends. The female ones do tapestry and have a cat. After a week or two at the job they can become very expert and all of them nurture secret hopes of being asked to become analysts for one or other of the new financial conglomerates at six-figure salaries.

In short, they are human. One successful entrepreneur — now chasing the biggest deals after modest beginnings — has recognised their humanity and their weaknesses and developed a system for defeating the press. At least, that is what it seems like. He has compiled three columns of buzz words which he keeps in the top right hand drawer of his desk — which he eases open at the mere sniff of a journalist. And some of them do — sniff that is. The columns are these:

1	2	3
Meaningful	Planning	Envelope
Constant	Environmental	Balance
Positive	Ecological	Proportions
Negative	Zonal	Improvement
Sound	Social	Infrastructure
Real	Fiscal	Mix
Formal	Tertiary	Parameters
Negotiable	Conceptual	Ambience
Basic	Procedural	Discipline
Fundamental	Progressive	Dialogue

The entrepreneur concerned litters his replies to journalists' questions with phrases made up at random — one word from each column in the order 1, 2 and 3. He never gets a bad press. Journalists reel away from his office staring unbelievingly at their notebooks — or, in the hubbub of their offices, replace their telephones after a mind-stretching conversation with him and decide to spend the rest of the day in El Vino's or the Wig & Pen.

As we have said before, no one is going to trouble you much if you curb your ambition. No one is going to waste column inches in *The Times*, *Daily Telegraph* or *Independent* on a two-up, two-down conversion in Acton — unless you uncover the decaying evidence of mass murder or treasure trove. And no entrepreneur worthy of the name would utter a whisper about either of these things. It would hold up the contract.

And, while we are on the subject of holding up the contract, it is probably worth mentioning the small matter of archaeological excavation — always fascinating to the British reading public avid for news of uncovered Viking ships, a scrap of Roman mosaic or the remains of a body or two. The archaeological lobby has carved quite a niche for itself in the development process. In areas where there is a fighting chance of finding something interesting, the developer is expected to allow archaeologists to swarm all over the site, digging holes, peering down them and occasionally clustering round some obscure remnant, all talking at once. And all of this at the developer's expense.

Redeveloping a twentieth-century site in Londinium, Deva or Camulodunum can be fairly traumatic. There, any developer who has bought a piece of land or a building can face delays. If the archaeologists find something — please don't let them find anything — delay can stretch into infinity. One developer has his own private archaeological consultant who can argue with the other archaeologist about the merits of the finds. There is always another point of view. If there isn't — and everybody argues that the find is the sensation of the century — the developer might just as well get down the hole and stay there.

However, if, quite apart from all that, you insist on climbing the entrepreneurial ladder to the top, you must be prepared to face the media — and, one day, a property journalist might actually win that coveted Pulitzer Prize for investigative journalism. And, just think, you might be his subject.

And don't ignore the local press. Every building you choose to develop — no matter how big or how small it might be — sits in the circulation area of a local newspaper. Editors of local newspapers are usually influential people who know everybody else of influence in the town. They are often members of the Rotary Club and a dozen other organisations which might have a positive point of view. Reference has already been made to the process of public consultation in planning. If the local

newspaper doesn't like what you plan to do, you obviously
have a problem.

These days, there is usually more than one local newspaper — even if the second or third is one of those free circulation newspapers known as 'freebies'. Although they are
primarily vehicles for local advertising — at a ratio of about
one square inch of editorial to every square foot of advertising — their front pages seek to carry some eye-catching
story. It could be yours. So the local press — like so many other
organisations and individuals with which you must treat — has
to be wooed, courted and, hopefully, seduced. If you have
reached the big league and your development portfolio is wide-
spread, the national press, the regional press, the local press,
the property press, the specialist press and all the rest have to
be wooed, courted and seduced.

And there is the increasing ethnic press. This usually has a
very positive opinion about most things and your building will
be no exception. Your wooing, courting and seduction may,
therefore, have to be conducted in Hebrew, Ibo or Urdu. And
then there is *Private Eye*. Try to keep out of it. Appearance in
the columns probably won't do your business reputation any
harm but it can play havoc with your private life.

And, as we have said before, this is quite another story.

It has been made clear that governments and local authorities often get things dramatically wrong — sometimes for the right and very commendable reasons. Things have a nasty habit of getting out of hand and governments — both national and local — are then compelled to take everything very seriously and promise action.

The inner cities problem is a case in point. The problem has to be solved as a matter of urgency — and the urgency is expressed and the action is promised as though the problem appeared overnight. The problem did not appear overnight. Some people forecast the problem as long as forty years ago when the New Towns Act was passed. Admittedly, there weren't many protesters and their relatively puny voices were discounted as the New Towns movement began to roll. But the idea of stripping inner cities of young families — the strong and the healthy — and jobs was labelled by some as totally wrong. They were visionaries of the wrong kind and, politically, at the time, their views were unacceptable.

And, of course, they weren't entirely right even though today they can say that they told us so. The New Towns movement, in general terms, was right for its time. Many thousands of young families have found happiness and relative prosperity in their new environments. Yes, there were complaints — complaints about architectural sameness, environmental sterility, people moving in advance of work availability. The residents who had lived for generations in designated areas resented the newcomers and argued bitterly against the new soulless estates. As a few pundits had said, it was all to be expected. But new communities — like problems — don't happen overnight either. (Well, that's not quite true. Some problems *do* happen overnight — but not the kind of problems we're talking about.) Communities have to grow. Towns and cities in this country have taken centuries to mature — to fashion themselves into balanced communities.

The critics were right to be concerned about pulling people and jobs out of the inner cities. Yes, there were international influences. World economics pulled and pushed at our industrial base. But the major cities that were to be robbed of people and jobs had, and it is worth repeating, taken centuries to grow. They had found their balance and, no matter how badly housed people were or how few jobs there were, transfer to satellite towns could only be a short-term solution. We were, as usual, putting off the evil day.

Then there were other influences. The influx of the ethnic minorities was, probably, the most significant — and the long-term effect of that was forecast in a highly-publicised speech in Wolverhampton which most of us thought was shocking but probably right. The immigrants gravitated towards the central areas where jobs were few but, because of the earlier exodus, shelter was available and relatively cheap.

Quite apart from people, there was traffic. Central areas were clogged solid with motor cars — and then someone invented containerisation which made matters suddenly and dramatically worse. The influences weren't only big — like people and traffic and deteriorating buildings. They were often small and aerosol shaped. Environmental deterioration was undoubtedly accelerated by the aerosol. You can see the effects on newly painted walls on the underground — indeed, on anything which stands still long enough to squirt at. Add to this the occasional riot and you have the beginnings of an inner cities problem.

And then, of course, there was politics. Some local authorities — for all the right reasons as they saw them — put muscle into welfare services and housing. They spurned the office blocks and shopping centre — and, in doing so, knocked another nail into the central area coffin. Today, we have the knock-on effect of all this. It should come as no surprise. It wasn't sudden like an earthquake. It grew steadily from a mix of political action and inaction and international and national economics and migration. It has been lurching towards us — very visibly — for the last thirty or so years.

What we have now, they say, is opportunity. For all those derelict acres, all this disintegrating housing, all those empty workplaces, can be re-vitalised — as a joint venture between the public and private sectors.

If you have been paying attention, you will know that the developer — whether he is just budding or in full flower — is concerned about costs and yields — yields in terms of both revenue or — even and/or — capital growth. He has to be. Even if the developer doesn't have shareholders, he normally has someone to whom and for whom he is responsible. We mentioned the problem of the awful failure returning home to Mile End to explain to the little woman where the life's savings had gone. We can call it simply the profit motive. There can be no philanthropists in the development business — at least, not until they have made their umpteenth million and then they can be as philanthropic as they wish and they usually are.

It is all a matter of scale. No matter how enormous the problems seem to be — and, let there be no mistake about it, the problems are vast — there is a place for every kind of developer in the inner cities. For the big and the small and the middling, this — the inner city — is the place of opportunity.

We can start at the top because it is the most exciting. If you are prepared to spend a billion or two, you will be surprised at what fringe benefits you can set aside for the community — and still make enough profit to appease the shareholders. Even on a relatively small scale, developers have been known to build clinics, libraries, car parks and community halls at no cost to the public purse — and still make a handsome enough profit on their schemes. If that is possible on schemes costing twenty million pounds, you can imagine what can be achieved on the very large.

All that is needed is recognition by some of the more militant local authorities — and, not surprisingly, militancy is strongest where the problems are the greatest — that the very big developers are not as evil as history and property mythology would have us paint them. They have confidence in themselves but, more impressively, they have the confidence of those with bags and bags of uncommitted money which would otherwise lie idle — idle, that is, in inner city terms. Certainly, without the very big developers, this money would be unlikely to be directed in the right quantities towards the inner city problem. The rich investors need to have confidence and don't always have confidence in government-inspired initiatives. Give them a commercial leader with a strong track record and they will stump up the millions to back his ideas. Commercial space could be the reason for the up-grading of hard to let residential space. An office block here, a shopping parade there and all kinds of new facilities could spring up to bind the communities together — or, better still, blend them in a new harmony. Already, there are plans afoot on a gigantic scale — and there is clear benefit in regeneration terms.

And you, budding developer, can play your part. Take on the improvement and conversion of a terrace of decrepit villas and make them once again into homes for which there is a demand. The work does not always have to reach the standards required by the gentrification brigade — although there will always be opportunity for that. Initiatives in the housing field are not new but there is, in the 1990s, unparalleled opportunity to improve the housing stock.

If you remember, reference has been made to the hugger-mugger nature of urban growth. It was natural for shops, houses, workshops, small factories, studios and all manner of things necessary to a community to grow up side by side. Only the planners and the new towns sought segregation on a total scale. There is now every chance to encourage a new mix of uses — perhaps not the old hugger-mugger that many of us remember but cosy and human as it should be. It will not have escaped your notice that, interspersed with the often not so profitable housing, could be commercial space of a size and

form to match local demand. So long as you have done your research, of course.

We could, between us, offer some advice to government. Every inner city with a problem — and not every inner city has one — could be declared a gigantic enterprise zone with all kinds of expedited procedures if we need any procedures at all, grants, rate-free periods, no planning control to speak of and a co-operative local authority. That would really get us all moving.

Although the inner cities are expressed as a major problem, as has been said, there is no problem in many of them. After all, Mayfair and Belgravia are inner city locations and the major problems there have rather more to do with the fact that some light-fingered visitors have a mania for collecting Spirits of Ecstasy or Silver Ladies from the bonnets of unattended Rolls-Royces. A whole new industry has grown up to protect, replace or replicate them which just shows what opportunities exist for enterprise in what must be a limited market.

The point is that there is opportunity everywhere. Certainly, it will exist aplenty in the inner cities and you will be urged to play your part. But it exists in every market town, every suburb, every village and, if you remember, out in the country where there is surplus farmland and redundant buildings. So, if you must and you still want to be a developer, get to it.

If you remember page 70 (I know it's not easy to recall every gem this book contains), we discussed the problem of betterment. Betterment — or improvement of value — has a particular significance in the innner cities. In fact, it is something of a problem. The present rash of Secretaries of State and Ministers of the Crown don't actually recognise it as a problem. I know that because I have talked to them about it. Indeed, one or two of the more illustrious (or infamous) don't actually understand it at all and they serve on the Cabinet Committee on inner cities. On the other side of the political fence, those once so anxious, so keen, that society should share in the benefits of a planning permission have no proposals in their latest policy documents. I have talked to them about it too. Of course, the new, voter-friendly socialism is just as much based on a free-market philosophy as Thatcher radicalism. But all of them should really try to understand this problem of value improvement. If they don't or can't — and nothing is, therefore done about it — the whole regeneration game in the inner cities will be stifled.

The assumption — certainly on my part — is that inner cities are for people. Many people in inner city locations live in sub-standard housing which could do with a few modern amenities or the houses could be cleared away and better buildings provided. If public or private money is invested in a major building — say an office block or even a cultural centre of some kind — the land and buildings around it rise in value. The next building has the same effect. Values jog upwards. Ah, say the free marketers, but the values of the houses rise too. That is true, but only in a locational sense. They are still the same tatty houses they were yesterday. They need money spent on them to make them fit — and such is the pattern of investment that the only way they can attract improvement is through gentrification. If that happens, up go land and building values again. The real people can no longer afford what is available.

London's Docklands suffered the rising value syndrome. You can speak to the people who once lived there and have had to move in with Aunt Bessie, because they could no longer afford to stay. There are quite a few of those. If inner cities are for people rather than office blocks, there has to be recognition that, if those people are to have good housing, someone has to pay for it. There just has to be a massive subsidy from somewhere — but from where? Not from the local authorities, they are being rate capped. Not from the housing associations, they rely mostly on Government money through the Housing Corporation and there is not enough of that. From the Government then? Neither of the main parties recognises it as a problem – remember?

Even if thousands of houses were built by the public sector, present policies and laws give the lucky tenanats the right to buy. Sit tight during the pre-emption period while values rise and the tenants are on to a winner. You can see the muddles we can get ourselves into.

The budding developer can sleep soundly in the knowledge that none of this is his concern. The present policies — and, so far as one can judge, the future policies as well — offer only opportunity for exploitation.

13 DIY DEVELOPMENT FOR WIDGET MAKERS

A high proportion of commercial and industrial space in this country is owner-occupied. This harsh fact is depressing enough for the property owning developers but, at the same time, it can be quite depressing for the owner-occupiers themselves if they don't know what to do with it should they wish to expand or relocate. Property ownership brings its own batch of responsibilities.

If you are preoccupied with all that goes into the manufacture of widgets or marmalade, you can be excused for not knowing much about property. There are very few property developers who understand the purpose and manufacture of widgets. But owner-occupiers, whatever they do for a living, have the capacity and normally the need to exploit their assets, to bolster their balance sheets or expand their businesses.

We have said earlier that most owner-occupiers, these days, have a clearer understanding of the value of their buildings. Their understanding of the rest of the problems surrounding their property is, however, fairly blurred. Nevertheless, each and every owner-occupier has the capacity to be a do-it-yourself developer. Like the professional developers, he doesn't have to use his own money. He needs only two things — an objective and the right advice.

It must be clear to the reader by now that there is money in abundance available for anything that looks sensible. As might be expected, the property professionals have dreamed up all manner of financial and procedural devices — with a matching glossary of terms — to suit the owner-occupier who has space problems.

There might be a whole package of problems — even opportunities. If an owner-occupied factory site has space for extension, it might just have enough space to go one better and provide another factory for sale or letting to somebody else. This adventure in speculation could pay for the owner-occu-

pier's own extension — and, perhaps, even leave some change for re-tooling or a few extra condiments in the staff dining-room. No matter how aware a board chairman may be of his property assets, he may not have thought of that little wheeze.

There is something called sale and leaseback. Imagine that you, as a do-it-yourself developer, own and occupy an office block which needs modernisation. It is adequate but fails to match the image of your success. You are half aware that the space planners could create a more efficent working environment and provide more working space for the expansion you expect. All of this would cost money. You could borrow it from the bank. You would then have to orchestrate the whole refurbishment and space planning process — all those planners, architects, surveyors, quantity surveyors, structural engineers and all the rest. Don't forget the ten per cent rule which might apply. With that extra ten per cent and the space you might save through re-planning, you might even produce some surplus space which you could let — through letting agents and the marketing people. That is quite a lot of work. You may have to bring in management consultants to make sure that your work is flowing in the right direction. If you do all of this successfully and your covenant is good (which, of course, it is), you could sell the freehold of your offices to an investing institution and pay rent. The price you are paid could be staggering. You could have enough to re-tool your factory if you have one or, if you fancy a four months' rest, make multiple applications for shares under false names.

That is what sale and leaseback is all about. You lose the value of the freehold for balance sheet purposes — but that could, at least, make you less vulnerable to takeover bidders who only love you for the potential of your property assets anyway. You do, of course, have to pay rent and probably service charges to the new owner — and rent reviews usually only move in an upwards direction every three or five years. But you have a building which matches your image and fits your present and foreseeable needs. What is more, you have money in the bank for whatever purpose you choose to use it.

Although rent and rates are, these days, a significant overhead, they are for most companies a relatively small proportion of administrative cost. Rents may have spiralled — but so have salaries, pensions, national insurance, BUPA and the cost of running company cars. It is a matter of making a judgement about the value of an appreciating asset in the balance sheet compared with a great heaving pile of liquidity.

That judgement is, of course, yours. Only you can make it

because only you properly understand your aspirations and the financial needs of your company. If you decide to follow the sale and leaseback route, you need advice. Much will depend on the size and nature of the building and its location — but, in general terms, you could do no better than to go to one of the big surveying practices with plenty of skills and access to institutional funds looking for investment. They will have the capacity, quite apart from everything else, of project managing a refurbishment project. They can examine your needs in a dozen ways and, you never know, you could end up with another freehold in a much nicer location where you can sail for an hour every evening or have a round of golf before you go to the office. And still have a pile of cash in the bank from the sale of the original freehold.

The message is, of course, take advice. You may be a determined do-it-yourself exponent but stick to painting the nursery or putting up a shelf or two. It is not that you would necessarily do the property job badly. You might just fail to recognise all of the options — and lose the chance of exploiting what you have to the best advantage.

Some of today's leading property men started their careers outside the property industry. They ran a factory making this or that — maybe they owned more than one factory. They had surplus space or had some other property problem which introduced them to the property world. They took advice — and they are still surrounded by hosts of consultants, many of them with access to funds. The profits they made in their factories now pale into insignificance beside their present turnovers.

And that could be you. Sale and leaseback is not the only option. What you need is someone beside you who knows his way through the jungle; someone who has negotiated all those reefs and shoals before. The property world is a dangerous place but, if after taking advice you get your property problem right, you acquire a taste for it, you would be welcome in the property world. Overcrowded though it may be, there is always room for the practitioner who gets it right.

14 DOWNTURN, RECESSION AND OTHER HARDSHIPS

Although every effort has made to show that property development is no sinecure, no job for faint hearts, it has to be said that things can get worse — infinitely and dramatically worse. In fact, so bad can they become that suicide is not uncommon and bankruptcy is frequent. Grown men have been known to throw their executive toys through windows and even to forget to call on their mistresses on the way home. Some forget to go home at all — but most developers' wives have grown accustomed to that. In fact, some of them prefer it that way, particularly when things are bad. It is no fun living with a caged tiger, or a frustrated fat cat.

What irritates the developer most when things go wrong is that none of it is his fault. International economics, national economics, inept government, even competent government — all these things can cause a downturn in his fortunes.

Take, for example, the Government's fight against inflation. One way to fight inflation is to put up interest rates. As most of us are personal borrowers, even if only from a building society, we are affected by this. Our cost of living rises and, if we are members of a strong union, we bang in a wage claim. That affects the profitability of our employers unless they put up their prices, in which case they cease to be competitive. In these circumstances, they go out of business and their employees lose their jobs. If people lose their jobs, they can't afford to spend as much as they once did, and that causes an economic downturn. In the retailing sector, an economic downturn means less spending, so the retailers prune their workforces, reducing their outlets and don't give too much away in the form of special offers.

People become selfish, belligerent and turn on the government of the day. This is the stuff of revolution, even though it may only be expressed through the ballet box in due course.

All of this happens because interest rates are raised a point or two for, on the face of it, sound economic reasons. The ramifications are not only material; they are spiritual as well. The media make sure that everyone knows about the problems. Clever analysts tell us what dire misfortune — even disaster — is just around the corner. Trade figures, what happened in New York or Tokyo yesterday or this morning, the fact that yet another minister has left the Government in something of a pet, the news that Charles and Di are not hitting it off too well — all of this is blown out of perspective. The Stock Exchange, which swings between optimism and pessimism for what seem to a terrified observer to be the most naive of reasons, causes companies to crash. And if it isn't the Stock Exchange, it's the Fraud Squad tipped off by investigative journalists (still bent on that Pulitzer prize) who, by brilliant innuendo, point the finger of suspicion at everybody, including the janitor who was only emptying the waste bucket.

What it all does, of course, is to destroy confidence. It destroys everybody's confidence (except the party in opposition) but, most of all, it destroys business confidence. Normally adventurous entrepreneurs, accustomed to 18-hour days and the taking of risks, start drawing in their horns and sulking in their tents. No, they won't take that new office, factory or shop. This, they say, is no time for expansion. Read your newspapers, they say, it's all there in black and white and even the CBI seems to confirm it, although you can never be sure. They, too, begin to think of redundancies.

So where is the property developer in all this? In short, probably having a nervous breakdown. He began a large slice of his present development programme what seems like donkey's years ago. Don't forget all the procedures he had to follow, all the battles he had to win, just to get to the point of laying the foundations of his buildings. He has borrowed yards of money to get this far and is committed to borrowing yards more to finish the job. Suddenly, all his sums are knocked sideways by a rise in the base rate. If you happen to have borrowed £20 million, a 2% rise in interest means another £400,000 a year. If you are borrowing over an extended period, the number of noughts in the sum can make one a little fretful. Some very well respected developers have established lines of credit at fixed rates of interest, but you, the budding developer, cannot hope for the same consideration. You will probably have your own little bank where your own little bank manager has agreed to lend you what you need. It won't be £20 million necessarily, but what you borrow won't be at a fixed rate of interest either.

Your bank manager will have been reading his newspapers too. He will know exactly the trouble you are in and, because he has his own future to protect, he is probably ready to pull out from under your feet the very rug he provided for you just a few months ago when you bought him lunch. Any day now, he could say that he wants his money back or, as he will put it, call in the loan. That wouldn't be so bad in normal circumstances. But these are not normal circumstances. This is downturn; this is recession.

If it had been normal circumstances, you might have had your building pre-let to a tenant with an extraordinarily good covenant at an agreed rental which reflected the rising market. Your expert consultants, in the light of that pre-let, would probably have already agreed an onward sale to an investing institution really keen to have it at full value. You could then have returned to the bank manager the pittance you had borrowed, paid him all the interest he had demanded and still had enough for that villa in Marbella, or whatever it was that you had your eye on.

What tenant? What investing institution? When you really need them, tenants are twenty times worse than policemen at being conspicuous by their absence. But don't forget there is a downturn, a recession. Tenants have their problems too — and they too have been reading the papers which give them no reason for optimism, expansion or, indeed, to take your wretched building at its inflated rent. The investing institutions are no better. Many of them are insurance companies and, because of global warming or whatever reason there is for sudden surges of wind at 103 miles per hour, they have taken a financial battering themselves. They would rather stay liquid, thank you very much, and buildings in recession are just not liquid enough. The market is, as they say, stagnating, no movement, and algae grow on both the buildings and the 'for sale' boards. And you are stuck with your un-let or un-sold building, your debt and your fidgety, and by now totally neurotic, bank manager. Don't worry too much about him; your own neuroses will be active enough.

It would be wrong to overstate the conditions inherent in downturn and recession. Nevertheless, many experienced developers find themselves in just the position described. They have years — indeed, by the look of some of them, centuries — of experience. And yet, they too are caught with their trousers down, or whatever cliché tickles your fancy. All those years of experience and they still tumble. Yield figures soar, which means that capital values drop at an alarming rate. Suddenly, the developer and, worse, his bank manager realise that the collateral no longer supports the level of borrowing needed for the current development programme, which is unlikely to be let when it's finished anyway.

The larger property companies, which have been around for a few decades and which hold some prime buildings as investments, usually have enough fat to survive. Their chairmen may have an uncomfortable hour or two at shareholders' meetings or in front of quizzical property analysts, but they will survive. What are now called the 'trading' developers, those who build, let and immediately sell on, are less fortunately placed. All they have is massive company debt and a development programme which eats money. The lettability, and thus the onward sale, of their buildings when they are completed are open to serious doubt. What is surprising is that they can still raise a smile and the occasional glass of champagne.

The answer is, of course, as we all know, that property is cyclical. Those in property know that one must take the longer-term view. Everything will turn out right in seven or so years' time. That is all very well. It is not much good telling your bank manager that all will be well in 1998 when he, like everybody else, including the Government, is worried sick about tomorrow.

There is a suggestion that the cyclical nature of property is an artifical device invented by property people to frighten off the competition. If it is true, they have made a good job of their invention. Press reports that millions have been wiped off the value of somebody's property investment porfolio or from a property company's share value leave the aspiring developer seriously inclined towards bus-conducting or even doubling the size of the fruit and veg barrow in Mile End. Anything — but anything — to avoid having millions you don't have wiped off the value of developments you haven't finished and won't be able to let or sell anyway.

In truth, it is all a matter of time. Time will, sooner or later, turn the cycle from bust to boom again. That is what history teaches us — just as it teaches us that time will surely turn boom back into bust yet again when the constituents are right for that to happen. Time is important in the property industry. We referred to Peter Palumbo. It was Peter Palumbo's father who, slowly and methodically, built up his own ownership of the buildings facing the Mansion House, known as the Mappin and Webb Group. Twenty-five years later, his re-development dream is about to come true. Peter Palumbo has won his planning permission. He had to go to the House of Lords to get it, but by that time, he had become a Lord himself, although that had nothing to do with his planning achievement.

As bust turns to boom, it is to be hoped that the property developers and the professionals who serve them will remember the cyclical nature of their hardware. No over-staffing, no over-borrowing, no over-optimism. Bust is certainly round the corner. The trouble is that no one can judge precisely the radius of the curve.

It is one of those extraordinary things about successful developers that they seem to have come from nowhere. They burst into the limelight in a flash of publicity about some multi-million pound deal and the light remains on so long as the deals keep rolling. No one asks about their childhood, where or if they went to school, what sort of hobbies they had as youngsters — it is all the here and the now and what is likely to happen if they overstretch themselves. If the question is put at all, they produce biographical notes which certainly weren't written by Ian Fleming and which are about as informative as that brown paper bag we were talking about earlier.

Occasionally, it is possible to pick up a hint of the past. Most of the big names in property were — like all of us — kids with runny noses and holes in their socks, pants and jacket elbows. Ties, if they were worn at all, were askew and stained with indescribable alien substances. Hair was largely uncut and uncontrolled. They, like all of us, had spots and trouble with the matriculation or 'O' level examinations.

It is hard to find any who went to Eton or Harrow except to do Mum's shopping on a Saturday morning. Some seem to have been to university but not always for long. Parents were just as likely to have lived in a council house in Cleethorpes — and, certainly, few seem to have any claim to blue blood or silver spoons. There aren't many chinless wonders at the top.

The point of mentioning this at all is that there is actually no yardstick against which it is possible to measure your chances of success. It is, of course, reasonable to assume that, if you have come from nowhere, there is a real incentive to get somewhere.

There is, in all of the top people, an inner driving force — something which urges them on even when there is already enough in the bank to keep them in luxury for the rest of their lives and for several reincarnations thereafter.

So that is the first requirement — that almost indefinable driving force which keeps them going when, in personal economic terms, it doesn't matter any more. It is very real. It could come from the thrill of putting together bigger and bigger schemes — just to see the number of noughts stretched across the last page of the development appraisal. It could come from the desire to improve the environment, to create jobs, to put something back into society. For many of them — and this may come as a shock to their critics — this is now manifestly the only reason for going on. And, finally, the driving force could come from, simply, the fear of being bored to death and development is what they do best.

Certainly, they are not driven towards profit by a fear of hard work. One high-profile developer has been seen striding down London's Park Lane with a cordless telephone in each hand and he was actually talking into both of them. The pressure at the top is fierce. The pace in itself is destructive but, if you add to that the responsibility for ten digit projects, it is surprising that the top people sleep at night. Some of them don't, of course — well, not often. The negotiations on one major deal took an uninterrupted ninety-six hours — and the dealers on each side of the table took turns to have catnaps.

So, budding developer, if that is your ambition, you must be prepared to face that kind of music. Consider the heat and, if you can't stand it, get out of the kitchen or don't enter it at all. You can stick to your conversions in Acton or wherever it was and you can do very nicely — but you must realise that it is tough at the very top. The pace is frenetic.

The incompetence of successive governments has ensured a paucity of residential construction, a massive deterioration of the housing stock, an impoverished infrastructure and costs escalating to an extent that results in people buying smaller and smaller flats. For the budding entrepreneur, this is good news. Modest ambition will ensure a livelihood for the foreseeable future. The range of opportunity available is wide. It

should be possible — so long as ambition is kept on a tight rein — to work up a good, profitable business and a sizeable nest egg. If the budding entrepreneur sticks to residential conversions — with or without his barrow in Mile End — he should do very nicely. But, as we all know, developers are not like that. It is likely, if you have the development bug, that you are not like that either.

In fact, humanity is not like that. Humanity is skin, bones,

greed, lust, envy and hate. Humanity likes to go one better —
and, however happy the budding entrepreneur may be with
his flat conversion lot, he will have at least one eye cocked for
the big deal, the main chance. This will be the one, he thinks
(we can't keep saying she as well but no doubt she will be
about somewhere), which will make the proverbial fortune. It
will make enough for that villa west of Cannes, the pool, the
Rolls, the trimmings and enough in the bank to live on for
ever — although maybe not the reincarnations. But, when he
does that deal, it will not be enough. He will have acquired
the taste for big development — the risk, the hassle, the heart
pills. He might sit twitching at the pool's side for a fortnight
or so. And, in no time at all, he will be back. He will be back
to assemble sites, tangle with the Director of Aesthetic Design,
beat down the contractor and urge his letting agents on in the
purest Anglo-Saxon.

The true reason for all this must be clear enough. It is, in
short, the thrill of the chase — not the chase towards mere
riches but victory over the system. It is the system which is
the challenge. The planning jungle, reluctant lenders, temperamental architects leading or following the professional team
into dire uncertainty, recalcitrant contractors and letting agents
looking in quite the wrong direction. These add the spice to
the working day. It is the challenge which sets the blood
pounding in the ears and the pulse racing.

No top developer will admit to any of this. But ask their
wives or whoever their partners might be. If the developers
can be persuaded to take a short break in the Bahamas or
Bermuda, they become insufferable fidgets on the way to the
airport. They ring the office from Heathrow and make a nuis-
ance of themselves on the flight deck trying to contact London.
They suffer misery at their destinations because of the frus-
trations of the local telephone system. When they arrive at
their hotels, they enquire immediately about telex, telephone,
facsimile transmission and the times of return flights. They
whisk through the local equivalent of Yellow Pages for the

names of local architects, quantity surveyors and lawyers in case an urgent consultation is necessary. When wives unpack, they discover reams of paper where there should have been colourful, holiday shorts and files where there should have been rope-soled sandals. A cellular telephone is secreted inside the toilet bag.

They won't go into the water beyond their knees in case they fail to be recognised by the bearer of some vital message. They won't dine out, if they can help it, for the same reason. They complain every day about not getting yesterday's London papers until tomorrow — and they pounce on new arrivals for today's *FT*. They devour every word of it and snigger about a fall in somebody else's share prices — and then spend a sleepless night, pacing up and down on the sweltering verandah, worrying in case the fall should signal a general crash. After four days, sensible wives give up and everyone goes home for a rest. But not the developer. He will have arranged to be met at the airport by a fast car which whisks him off on a tour of development sites just to make sure they are all still there. They will be, of course. In fact, in four days, nothing will have changed — not even the site foreman's socks.

As someone was once in the habit of saying, do you sincerely want to do this? Development on a grand scale is a bug — a little green worm in the head which creates an obsessional craving to play with bricks and mortar, concrete and glass, on a massive scale. When cures have been found for everything else, the bug will still be there as virulent as ever. The important thing is never to let it take hold and the best way of doing that is to stick to those small residential conversions.

But, in truth, it is a strong man (or woman) who can resist the challenge to grow big; to build big and then bigger. And, also in truth, there will always be opportunity. We have mentioned all those 1960s buildings deserving of redevelopment. All of those shopping centres in need of updating to match shopper aspiration, all those sites in the Green Belt inviting the attention of the bulldozer. There are still acres of docklands in London, Liverpool and a score of seaports just waiting for investment. And then there is inner-city regeneration — with developers being urged by governments, local authorities and urban development corporations to do something about the increasing problems — and we have been into all that.

And that's only the physical side. There is no limit to man's ability to create demand. There is no need to call in Saatchi and Saatchi for that. There was George Brown's office ban all that time ago. Just when everyone was beginning to worry about a declining offices market, somebody invented the Big Bang. The City of London's first draft plan was, to the developer, offensively conservationist and wise pens quickly drew attention to the need to preserve London's place as one of the world's leading financial centres. The revised version of the plan gave developers just a little more elbow room. Whether the Big Bang has subsided into a Weak Whimper is relatively unimportant. Someone, somewhere, will dream up good reasons for yet another spate of opportunity for the developer who has grown bigger and is determined to grow bigger.

Every day, some new building proposal is announced. Some of the latest projects make the NatWest Tower look relatively puny. There is major refurbishment opportunity in abundance — and there are acres of land housing disconsolate goats waiting for release by the planner's pen. Government has already directed attention towards those unneeded agricultural acres and redundant barns.

But it will have not escaped the budding entrepreneur's notice that, these days, most of the topmost developers — from wherever they might have come — are people of great determination. Some are chartered surveyors, chartered accountants or lawyers. Some have studied hard and long and stretched their minds to grapple with the problems they must face in their chosen careers. Some have done all of those things but some have not. But nearly all of them have formidable minds — with physical stamina to match. At the very top, few drink or smoke and many practise yoga. Some sit alone for hours in the lotus position with their minds escaping to the skies to solve problems faster than computers.

They are not all like that, of course. Some make the most amazing whoopee (if you remember the song) and can be seen in the early hours at Annabel's, drinking pink champagne with the whole chorus from the Prince of Wales Theatre. They are usually the ones who don't last — but they go down smiling.

Even the first group enjoys its trappings of success. Some have helicopters; some of them even fly them themselves. Some have their own aeroplanes — not Piper Cubs or Cessnas but jet-engined airliners equipped with every conceivable kind of tomorrow's office technology. Some even have a separate berth for the travelling secretary but that is not always regarded as necessary. All of them have expensive motor cars with chauffeurs who keep them polished like glass. None of this is necessarily gloating pretension. The aircraft save time and trouble on international journeys — and, in five or six hours on the way to the States, it is possible to get through a whole pile of work. The reason that there is a big car and a chauffeur is not just so that the developer can sit in the back looking out of the window. There is always work to do — even if it is just thinking of where to raise the next billion pounds or two. And the yacht in Cannes' harbour is, arguably, a legitimate business expense because it can impress the bank manager in a way which nothing else can.

It has to be said that this kind of crash-bang-wallop lifestyle can bring some complications. There was a time when new-found riches turned a few heads — towards leggy blondes and the casinos at Monte. If that is what you want, it is easy enough. Many long-established marriages exploded into nothing — although it wasn't always the developer who was at fault in infidelity terms. He was far too busy — far too interested in cubic feet, mixed uses and land assembly. Sometimes, he just didn't get home for a week or two — and sometimes, he just forgot. Even long-established marriages can't take too much of that — and, often, it was the wives who got bored.

Before the crash of 1973/4, an innocent charity worker arranged a dinner for top property people — in the hope that they might put some of their millions into his charitable kitty. He spent hours working out the table plan and then thought he should check it with someone who really knew the property world. He thought that those with common interests should sit together. The advice he received could make a book in itself. Certainly, it caused total re-planning of the table. *This* developer couldn't sit beside *that* developer because *he* had just run off with *that* developer's wife. And *he* is now living with *his* ex-mistress. And *that* one is living with *that* one's daughter and is old enough to be her grandfather — and the father doesn't think much of it. The way the original plan had been drawn would have been a charitable disaster.

But all of that was a long time ago. The property entrepreneurs of today only have time to worry about their development projects — even if they had the inclination for anything else. That point has to be made — at the insistence of the present-day property entrepreneurs.

The budding entrepreneur, if he insists on hitting the big time, would be wise to emulate the first group. There are courses — means of education to the highest standard. There are methods of personal discipline which can create cool and expanding minds. And, when the going gets really tough — when the Director of Aesthetic Design, supported by all the conservationist and preservationist groups he can muster, rejects your proposals for the refurbishment and extension of some Victorian folly — there is always arson.

As Bertolt Brecht once said 'Grub first; then ethics.' Just get on with those flat conversions. Eventually, we might see you at the top.

INDEX

[183]

The Mercury titles on the pages that follow may also be of interest.
All Mercury books are available from booksellers or, in case of
difficulty, from:

Mercury Books
Gold Arrow Publications Ltd
862 Garratt Lane
London SW17 0NB

Further details and the complete catalogue of Mercury business
books are also available from the above address.

Edward Erdman

PROPERTY

Foreword by the Rt Hon Christopher Patten, MP

A CBI Initiative 1992 book

Most major business decisions have a property connotation and, although property is not a subject addressed by the Single European Act, it will have an important role in determining strategies for 1992.

As businesses consider expansion in the single market, they need to assess the availability and cost of acquiring new manufacturing bases, retail outlets, office and residential premises, and whether purchase, leasing or renting will provide the best returns. They need to take into account the different factors which may have a bearing on how and where they want to take on the new site: planning and building regulations, forms of tenure, taxation, grants available, the state of the construction market, the retail market, transport facilities and so on. Edward Erdman provides a detailed analysis of each of the member states' current position.

£17.95 (hardback)   **ISBN 1–85251–052–8**

Nick Thornely and Dan Lees

HOW TO BE A WINNER

Most of us want to be winners – which isn't too surprising as 'winners tend to be happier and more exciting than other people and, while they may or not be richer, their lives have a sparkle that losers can never experience'. Are you a winner? People in top jobs sound as if they should be winners but although presidents and monarchs hold the world's top jobs some of them have definitely not been winners.

How to be a Winner shows how to identify the real winners: the winning president, the winning executive, the winning secretary or the winning doorman. It will also help you spot a winning company, a winning team or a winning country. Nick Thornely and Dan Lees – both winners in their very different ways – maintain that in the game of life, as opposed to sporting contests, everyone can be a winner and that a winning company, for example, should be staffed by winners from the newest recruit up to the chairman. Enjoyment, they maintain, is the key factor in developing the winning habit. If you are ambitious, enjoying what you do could take you right to where you can do the most good for yourself and your company while stress is strictly for losers.

This amusing and thought-provoking look at the way we live and work will annoy the 'more than my job's worth' employee and the 'you're not here to think' type of employer, but the rest of us may well find that being a winner is more important than we realised. Winning – and helping other people to win – is what life is all about, all of which makes it essential to know *how to be a winner*.

'*Packed with confidence-boosting ideas*' ... **Executive Development**

£6.99 (paperback)   ISBN 1–85252–059–0

Barrie Pearson

COMMON-SENSE BUSINESS STRATEGY

How to improve your profits and cash flow dramatically.

Millions of managers and business owners have read books or attended seminars on strategy. Few people actually do manage their business strategically and they tend to have become millionaires!

Planning techniques have become so complicated that they are the preserve of 'planning experts'. The result has been long-winded business plans filed and forgotten almost as soon as they have been written.

Successful managers use strategic common-sense, not complex planning techniques. *Common-Sense Business Strategy* shows you how to create your own success story by achieving a 'quantum jump' improvement in results.

This book is based on more than ten years' successful experience of advising businesses ranging from household-name multinationals to unquoted companies and professional partnerships. *Common-Sense Business Strategy* tells you what to do, how to do it, and where to start. It is a book for those who want to manage strategically, and not simply read about it.

Common-Sense Business Strategy reveals . . .

- **How to Manage Strategically, using Common Sense**
- **How to Lay the Foundations for Success**
- **How to Take Stock of your Market Place**
- **How to Take Stock of your Company's Performance**
- **How to Develop a Vision to Ensure Success**
- **How to Overcome Obstacles to Success**
- **How to Develop Major Alternatives**
- **How to Make Successful Acquisitions**
- **How to Turn Around Loss-making Companies**
- **How to Hold a Strategic Workshop**
- **How to Make the Vision become Reality**
- **How to Make Successful Management Buy-outs and Buy-ins**

£14.95 (hardback)   **ISBN 1–85251–050–1**